till
SEX
do us part

till SEX do us part

make your MARRIED SEX irresistible

Dr. Trina E. Read

KEY PORTER  BOOKS

Library and Archives Canada Cataloguing in Publication

Read, Trina E.
Till sex do us part : make your married sex irresistible / Trina E. Read.

ISBN 978-1-55263-999-3

1. Married women—Sexual behaviour. 2. Wives—Sexual behaviour.
3. Sex in marriage. I. Title.

HQ29.R42 2008   646.7'8   C2007-905479-X

The CANADA COUNCIL | LE CONSEIL DES ARTS
FOR THE ARTS | DU CANADA
SINCE 1957 | DEPUIS 1957

ONTARIO ARTS COUNCIL
CONSEIL DES ARTS DE L'ONTARIO

The publisher gratefully acknowledges the support of the Canada Council for the Arts and the
Ontario Arts Council for its publishing program. We acknowledge the support of the Government
of Ontario through the Ontario Media Development Corporation's Ontario Book Initiative.

We acknowledge the financial support of the Government of Canada through the Book Publishing Industry Development Program (BPIDP) for our publishing activities.

Key Porter Books Limited
Six Adelaide Street East, Tenth Floor
Toronto, Ontario
Canada M5C 1H6

www.keyporter.com

Text design and electronic formatting: Alison Carr
Illustrations: John Lightfoot

Printed and bound in Canada

09 10 11 12 13 5 4 3 2 1

For Dennis and Andrew, the loves of my life

CONTENTS

INTRODUCTION

Confessions of a Sex Expert Who Didn't Like Sex

When anyone asks what makes me a Sex Expert, they might see a tiny look of terror cross my face. I'm certain they've glimpsed through my cool façade and seen that deep down inside, I'm an uptight girl from small town nowhere who is clearly trying to figure this all out. Sure, I've been teaching women how to enjoy sex for a while and have a graduate degree in sex (can you imagine, schools giving out graduate degrees in sex?), but that doesn't mean the topic of sexuality doesn't befuddle me a lot of the time.

Not in a million years did I expect this to become my career. I spent the first ten years of my working life pushing paper, barely functioning in the stable 9-to-5 corporate world. In my late twenties, by chance I saw sex educator Sue Johanson give a speech. She tossed body parts, sexual positions, and safe-sex practices around like she was talking about the weather. I was enthralled. On her heels, Eve Eisler's *Vagina Monologues* took my hometown by storm. I went to the performance only because my friend was in the play and bullied me into going. I watched the entire performance slack jawed, as women boldly gave their vaginas names, and shared their good, bad, and ugly experiences. I walked away from that play with a yearning to be that open and free with my sexuality.

Within a year, as fate would have it, I had been fired from my nice cushy job. Instinctively I knew it was time to push the safe corporate career to the side and pursue this crazy idea of becoming a sex educator and sex coach (not a sex counsellor or therapist). As an educator I write and talk to thousands of women all over the world; as a coach I help couples bring the sizzle back into their relationships. Quite simply, I was scared beyond measure, unsure how it was going to turn out. Yet with a newfound fire in my belly, I took the plunge.

I wish I could say, "Then I lived sexually happy ever after." But I can't. Somehow I naively figured becoming a Sex Expert automatically guaranteed I would turn into a sex diva effortlessly having hot passionate encounters every night of the week. Surprise! Just over a year into my marriage, the daily grind of our relationship reality set in; I discovered, and was challenged with, the same sexual troubles of every super-busy woman. In fact, I was the poster child for learning the hard way how to make sex in a long-term relationship work.

There I was perched stiffly on a marriage counsellor's couch as my husband of three years complained, "Trina never wants sex anymore." We left the counsellor's office hurt, humiliated, and not speaking to one another. When we were getting ready for bed, I watched as my husband undressed in a huff and stomped to the bathroom to brush his teeth.

At that unforgettable pinnacle moment, confused feelings swirled through my head. As I stared at his naked bottom disappearing into the bathroom, I was keenly aware how sexually attracted I was to him. Even though there were days I wanted to toss him in the garbage and be done with it all, I truly loved him and desperately wanted to make this marriage work. We were sexually compatible and shared some wickedly wonderful and memorable sexual times together. I did enjoy sex—when I was in the mood. Yet my husband was right, for the last year of our marriage I hardly ever felt like having sex. And I couldn't figure out for the life of me how I'd gotten myself into this mess.

I was certain the universe had made me the brunt of a very cruel joke. Memories of many nasty breakups over a lack of sex came flooding back to me. Ironically, one of the reasons I became a Sex Expert was so this would never happen to me—again.

"Well," I thought, "It makes sense. I'm a super-busy woman flying all over the world speaking and writing, while trying to finish a graduate degree. My marriage has been tightly wedged on the bottom rung of my priority list." Smugly I—the new and improved Sex Expert—convinced myself all I had to do was "Get back on that horse and ride."

With unabashed zeal I went to work and did all the good and sensible things a few sex books told me: communicate, schedule sex, and create a romantic environment. But with every sexual encounter the sex only got worse. Mortified, I began blaming my aging libido for a lack of sexual interest; however, medical tests proved my hormones were at a normal level. It became obvious there was a missing link to me having great sex and, frustratingly, I didn't have a clue what it was.

I felt indescribable shame. People would give me a wink and a nod and say, "Sex Expert, eh? Your husband must be a very happy man." In my misery I would respond with a weak smile and think, "No, he's not. Truth be told, I'm a big phony. Here I am, an absolute walking encyclopedia of sex, and I can't even keep the sex in my relationship together."

Thankfully just as my marriage and self-esteem were about to be flushed down the toilet, I realized the truth: I wasn't alone in my shameful sexual secret. (Why is it so much easier to diagnose someone else's problem rather than your own?) On my speaking tours around the world, hundreds—maybe thousands—of couples had described the same issue to me. Indeed, I had no doubt at that moment millions of super-busy couples experienced the same predicament. In fact, some studies show that there are more than forty million women who report these kinds of difficulties.

I became a woman with a monstrously huge mission. Two years later, after reading piles of books and scholarly journals, writing newspaper and magazine columns, rolling this problem around in my head, and talking to multitudes of couples, everything clicked into place. The answer was simple. Since the average super-busy married woman (not presenting a sexual dysfunction) only ever learned to have what I call "single-woman sex" (you'll learn all about this in Chapter 1) with little to no intimacy, she was unable to enjoy the sexual act as much as she could, or would, like.

Consequently, sex became a chore or one more thing on her to-do list. To turn her situation around, she first needed to turn the negative emotions she felt toward sex to positive ones; only then could she begin to have married-woman sex. To do this, she needed a big dose of sexual self-confidence. (Although the book refers to "married women" it applies to any woman in a long-term relationship who seeks to improve her sex life.)

To be sure I was on the right track I wanted to test my theory. A friend of mine said her mommies group would be happy to be my guinea pigs. I tentatively bumbled my way through the theory of single-woman sex versus married-woman sex. You could have heard a pin drop; almost every face showed "This is exactly what's happening in my bedroom." I knew in that instant I was onto something big.

Please take heart, *I am convinced that keeping your busy lifestyle and having a healthy sexual relationship is not only possible, but also doesn't mean completely changing your life to make it work.* Creating married-woman sex in your relationship means incorporating a small cluster of doable things that will eventually add up to a lifetime of great sex.

While writing this book I became pregnant and had a beautiful baby boy. Even though my career is as busy as ever, with the added pressures of being a new mom, I'm happy to report sex and intimacy with my husband are great. And no it doesn't mean we're having hot and crazy sex every night, but when sex does occur it's fun for both of us. More importantly, I look forward to the next time we can get together. The thing is, I've just followed my own advice. It's made me believe even more strongly that I've cracked the why-married-women-don't-like-sex code. Regardless of how busy you are, or whatever stage your sex life is at, this book will help you move into a successful sex life.

Till Sex Do Us Part offers many ideas and approaches to sexuality. Why? There are so many variables to your specific situation—which differ from any other couple's sexual situation—that a one-size-fits-all, fix-it approach to creating a new and better sexual relationship is unrealistic. I hope that by offering a smorgasbord of ideas, you can pick and choose what works with your sex life to put it back on track.

Getting your sex life back doesn't have to be complicated; however, it does mean at least a minimum commitment from you and, hopefully, your partner. It's essential to select ideas that will work for your present lifestyle and situation. Sexual challenges that aren't covered in this book can be found in the Resources section; you'll find books and websites relating to depression, menopause, erectile dysfunction, medications, and the like.

Watch for the ideas in this book that push your buttons (i.e., whoever feels like having sex less is in control of the sex). If you find yourself getting mad, it's probably something you need to investigate, work through, and resolve. Chances are until you resolve what is upsetting you, your sex life won't be able to resurrect itself. As well, although I do appreciate it took both of you to create this sexual dynamic and it needs a commitment from you both to work things out, this book is written for women. The purpose of this book is to give you the courage and moxie to create a sex life that works for you.

Most importantly, although I know you want to immediately turn your sex life around with a flick of your multi-tasking wrist, pick only one thing to start with. Work on it, make it an unconscious habit, and then progress to the next. Working on your sex life is not a 100-metre sprint; it's a lifelong marathon. Relax, enjoy the ride; time is on your side.

Good luck and many blessings for a happy, healthy relationship.

OVERVIEW

Before you begin reading the book, let me explain my method of getting your sex life back on track. It follows a very specific step-by-step agenda: why your sex went wrong; ideas that will help fix it; and how to create the sex life you want.

Chapter 1: You Like Sex and Your Partner But ...

Here's the single-woman sex versus married-woman sex concept. It will give you insight into the many reasons why sex has gone sideways in your relationship. As well, it's an opportunity to see early on if the book's concept fits with what is going on your sex life.

Chapter 2: Getting Real with Your Single-Woman-Sex Situation

The first step moving into married-woman sex is to take responsibility for why sex has gone south in your relationship. I'm not saying that it's entirely your fault or yours to fix. But sex is a team sport and as half of this team you have to start figuring out why you aren't enjoying sex as much as you could.

Chapter 3: Getting Rid of Your Single-Woman-Sex Baggage

The second step , once you take responsibility, is to ditch your negative emotions around sex. The reason many women don't want sex isn't about the physical act itself, it's about all the negative feelings that have built up over time.

Chapter 4: Talking to Him about Sex

The third step is to learn how to assertively communicate through the issues that are getting in the way of sex. It means having an open, honest, and ongoing dialogue. As productive communication is the number-one downfall for couples, this chapter is full of communication guidelines, tips, and tools. In fact, we'll troubleshoot what to do if he doesn't take the news of your new sex life well.

Chapter 5: Creating the Sex Life That You Want

Once you become effective at assertive communication, step 4 is to tell your partner what you want out of the sexual experience. Good sex starts with defining what you want out of your sexual experience. This chapter will help you create a plan to get your sex life back on track.

Chapter 6: Your Sexual Needs are Equal

In order for you to be an equal inside the bedroom, step 5 is you building emotional intimacy and sexual self-confidence outside the bedroom. Sex needs to become a day-to-day positive experience. This chapter provides a list of small daily habits you do outside the bedroom that will create and facilitate the much needed nurturing and intimacy between you and your partner.

Chapter 7: Making Your Body Your Sexual Ally

Step 6 is to understand how your body works. Listening to your body's unique sexual rhythm, instead of being a floating head, is your one-way ticket to enjoying sex more.

Chapter 8: Having Sex on Your Terms

Once you've created intimacy outside the bedroom and have your body tuned into great sex, step 7 is creating great sex habits inside the bedroom—on your terms. No longer do you wait for your partner to decide when and how sex will happen; you boldly instigate the sex you want. You'll also learn how to get your sexual momentum going and how to make it stay.

Chapter 9: Making Your Married-Woman Sex Stick

Now it's time to celebrate your success and play. Ongoing good sex means mixing it up, bringing novelty and never allowing things to get stale. This chapter presents ideas, tips, and techniques for how to keep sex a priority for many years.

CHAPTER 1

You Like Sex and Your Partner But …

"Anton and I thought we were special, somehow immune to love's travails but, in truth, we were nothing out of the ordinary, just another pair of souls who could not hold it steady when the going got tough."

—Marian Keyes, *The Other Side of the Story*

I want to let you in on a little secret. If you don't enjoy sex in your relationship right now, you're perfectly normal. In fact, why would you find your sex life satisfying? In my opinion, whoever coined the term "happily ever after" should be drawn and quartered. It's absolute lunacy that one day you'll meet your soulmate and then, shazam, the two of you will ride off into the sunset and be super sexual forever more. Yet, if this myth hadn't been perpetuated and we had known the truth, we humans might have died out long ago.

Be honest, if someone had sat you down and told you exactly what your sex life was going to be like after only a few years of life together, you might have turned on your heel and run away screaming. In fact, a lot of people have decided to say no to long-term relationships; divorce rates have hovered at more than 50 per cent for a number of years. Irreconcilable differences involving sex or finances are two big reasons people split.

Let's assume you don't want to get a divorce; rather, your relationship is mostly happy except for the sex part. Once upon a time, you and your partner were having sex like bunnies and then one day you woke up next to someone who's more like a roommate than a lover. You love your partner and want to have a stronger intimate bond with him—you just don't know how. Having infrequent sex—in a society that puts so much value to self-worth on being sexy and sexual—is an uphill battle that millions of couples grapple with every day of their marriage.

Consequently, you're not alone if you've been searching for an easy solution to a complicated modern-life sex question: How can I have fun, fresh, and meaningful sex while trying to be super-mom, super-wife, super-worker, and oh yeah, finding some "me time"?

Indeed, your situation is probably similar to Stacey's. She wants to have more great sex with her husband—she just doesn't know how. Instead her hit-and-miss (mostly miss) sex life leaves her feeling resentful, guilty, and apathetic. Stacey is healthy, doesn't have a sexual dysfunction nor are her hormone levels out of whack. Consequently she's come to the conclusion that she has lost her libido. She doesn't realize that her libido has little or nothing to do with her desire to have sex.

She's an average woman whose sex life has fallen into the omnipresent sex trap: sex was amazing in the first few years of her relationship but since the kids, job, and everything else, sex has taken a back seat. She's simply really, really busy. As a result, Stacey spends more time avoiding sex than having it. Yet she adores her husband and desperately wants to keep their intimate connection.

There is a logical reason for Stacey's sex transformation. Too many married women keep having single-woman sex long after the "I do's."

Have you ever thought back to figure out how you learned the fine art of having sex? After reaching puberty, many young women and their girlfriends talked about sex a lot. Perhaps you read a Harlequin romance or two, then dog-eared and reread the juicy passages. You scoured *Cosmopolitan* with its monthly "25 Best Ways to Get Him Hot" articles while hiding from parental eyes.

Then you met your first special someone who made your heart—and other body parts—go pitter-patter. In your teen/young adult hormone–induced haze you fumbled your way through first, second, and third base, excited and scared at the same time. Even though you might not have had intercourse, how you were initiated, your ability to experiment without feeling stupid, and the short timeline to learn all about sex limited your sexual socialization.

The result was that you only ever learned how to have one type of sex, which I call single-woman sex. You probably never gave this way of having sex a second thought because with your short-term love affairs the single-woman-sex formula usually worked well. Maybe once or twice you saw glimpses of how your sex became less exciting as relationships faded into the sunset; however, before boring sex could become a reality, you moved on to the next steamy-hot relationship. And then one day a very special person came into your life and the short-term relationship became long-term.

Long-term relationships carry with them a different set of sex rules that, unfortunately, the happily-ever-after people neglected to inform you of. So, like most people, you went into your long-term relationship having the same type of single-woman sex over and over and over again. At the start, just like every other relationship, you had an invincible sex life and were doing better than perfectly fine, thank you very much.

So when after only two years of marriage, your sex life started going sideways, you and your partner understandably became confused. You had every good intention to maintain your sex life but it never seemed to work out; always something or someone getting in the way. You started to miss your intimate connection and wanted to be close again.

Problem was, you were already stuck in a comfortable single-woman sex rut. Your sex stayed stuck for many reasons: an inability to communicate your wants, needs, or desires; not knowing there was a different way; an inability to communicate sexual frustration; and a strongly held belief that once you met "the one" your amazing sex would magically last forever. Never addressing the change in sex, both of you watched helplessly as your sex life started to nose-dive.

Mini-fights, silent power struggles, and sarcastic little snipes about sex were never big enough to address as a "marital issue," but they definitely started chipping away at your sexual self-esteem. Unbeknownst to you, sex slowly became clouded by all the unconscious frustration, guilt, and anxiety under the surface. You rarely, if ever, resolved your negative feelings; you were simply too busy being busy and didn't want the hassle of working through a sticky issue. As well, neither you nor your partner knew how to productively deal with all the accumulating negative baggage. Choosing instead that when the lack-of-sex issue reared its ugly head, both of you either buried yours in the sand or had a knock-down-drag-'em-out fight.

Each sexual encounter became more and more like walking through a minefield. Sometimes you could forget all of those hurt feelings and let yourself get right into the sex. More often, though, you couldn't. Unwittingly, your feelings took your brain hostage and wouldn't allow your body to enjoy sex.

Not surprisingly, you developed a significant negative emotional pattern toward sex. Today, although most women in this situation can and do orgasm, you really don't enjoy sex like you used to. Instead, you go through the motions so you don't have to contend with the guilt and resentment hanging over your head.

Because you're reading this book, I assume you don't like your sexual state of affairs and want to turn it around. Take heart, making things better is possible.

IS IT INTERCOURSE OR IN YOUR HEAD?

When couples approach me for solutions to their sexual woes, they inevitably want "tips" on how to make their orgasm or intercourse more interesting and intense. They ask, "What are the best sex positions?";

"How can we find her G-spot?"; "What's the best vibrator?" and so on. While it's true sexual novelty does breathe life into a lacklustre sex routine (see Chapter 9 for tons of ideas), this is a "male" way of looking at sex—jump-start a lagging sex drive by having a bigger, faster, better orgasm. The hope is by experiencing a great orgasm, it will propel the couple to want more sex and thereby become closer and more intimate.

At this point, trying to fix the intercourse part of your relationship would be like putting a Band-Aid on an open wound.

So instead to start, you need to differentiate between the physical act of having sex and your emotional baggage. If you're a physically healthy woman (you can orgasm and/or when in the right frame of mind enjoy sex), it's not the intercourse mechanics you need to focus on; rather, you need to address the negative emotional baggage to help you out of your situation.

You see, it is only when you can once again feel positive toward sex that you can turn your sexual desire and sex life around. Once you toss the baggage, you can say "hello" to having a lifetime of well-deserved married-woman sex.

SEX WAS SIMPLE WHEN YOU WERE YOUNG BECAUSE ...

Do you remember how easy and exciting life was when you were young? Breaking free of parental ties and becoming independent. Carefree, you could hop in the shower and take two hours to get ready. Share an apartment with six other people, sleep on the floor, eat macaroni and cheese every night—because, of course, you had to save your money for important things like nightclubbing and purchasing a closet full of cheap clothes, fake jewellery, and makeup.

Okay, maybe this isn't exactly how your single-woman days were spent. Regardless, one of the many reasons sex was so exhilarating then is that you lived in a "romantic love" bubble. This bubble meant so much more than putting your best foot forward to impress your new love toy. Your romantic love bubble meant your world revolved around attracting inherently unstable relationships that ended before anything long term could develop; a month at worst, a year at best.

The instability kept you on your sex-always-has-to-be-at-its-best toes. Should you sleep with this person on the first date? Was he going to call you? If he didn't call five days after your first date, was he really interested? Or in other melodramatic vignettes, when things started going wrong, you played the ever-thrilling "come here, go away" game of breaking up and getting back together again.

What kept you in this instability loop?

When you meet someone you're attracted to, your hypothalamus (the part of your brain at the base of your skull about the size of the end of your thumb) sends signals to your body to start producing an impressive concoction of hormones that I like to call "love drugs." In fact Rutgers University anthropologist and author of *Why We Love*, Helen Fisher studies our romantic passion. She believes our instinct to love is similar to our drive for hunger and thirst.

Along with fellow researchers, Fisher used functional magnetic resonance imagining (fMRI) to peer into the brains of people in early stages of their relationship. When the test subjects looked at a photo of their partner, their brain's primordial centre, which floods the brain's dopamine-driven reward circuitry, registered an increase in activity. Dopamine is the brain's motivational chemical and is all about craving, elation, high energy and intensely focused attention, creates "highs" similar to those experienced on cocaine or speed, and suppresses production of serotonin, the hormone that helps stabilize our moods. The serotonin shortage creates the nonstop "can't get you out of my head" thinking. The brain's emotional and motivational zones become saturated with its own brand of amphetamines, which fire up feelings of intense romantic love.

These love drugs put you in a heightened state of arousal by kicking your libido into overdrive. When it comes time for you to have sex, you have to do very little for your body to get aroused. Your love hormones already have you good to go.

Add to this the fact that you likely came to the new love affair with your own bag of sex tricks. What does that mean? Almost every person has developed a special "sex move" they do well in the bedroom. You had yours and your partner(s) taught you theirs, giving you a pretty decent sexual repertoire. Having sex for the first little while with a new partner meant going into your little bag of tricks and deciding which sexual move you wanted to try. Being able to do all these new and exciting sex tricks for the first time together made you feel like two kids in a candy shop. And, not surprisingly, this novelty gave you enough sexual self-confidence to explore other techniques as well.

If that wasn't enough, you constantly wanted to impress him by preparing your mind, body, and spirit for the inevitable delicious time when you had sex. You always had a wax and polish (bikini wax and nail polish, that is), wore sexy underwear, and made sure your makeup was just so. He, in his infatuation, made sure his bedsheets didn't stink too badly and the bathtub was clean.

Therefore, it's easy to understand why, during the first six months, most couples get lost in a sex abyss. In an otherwise ordinary life, it's hard not to get addicted to feeling totally and utterly alive. And alive didn't always mean things were awesome in the relationship; it also meant crying in your glass of Chardonnay while your girlfriends consoled you because you were gaga about some bozo.

Even though, looking back at that time in your life, you would probably say, "Thank goodness, I never want to go through the dating scene again," every new encounter was an adventure.

Problem is, you're not hard-wired to live in constant relationship instability. In fact, as much as the mundane bores you to tears, your survival as a human being requires order, habit, and routine. Think back to the moment you knew you two officially became a couple; I bet both of you unconsciously moved forward to quickly create your couple routine. Initially experiencing that "at last" thrill of building a life together felt like you were being wrapped in a warm sweater.

However, by embracing the comfort and stability of a long-term relationship, we put the brakes on sexual excitement. Said anothᴇᴦ way, as the "will this relationship last?" uncertainty ebbed away and the daily grind took over, your sex likely became less and less interesting. Instead of being in a state of high anticipation, both of you were now seeing each other *au naturel* every day—you in your ugliest sweats, watching a show he can't stand; he scratching his crotch and farting—both of you completely oblivious to how this would affect your long-term sex.

Soon your warm-sweater feelings became a distant memory. Your single-woman-sex days that were so effortless no longer exist.

THE DIFFERENCE BETWEEN SINGLE-WOMAN SEX AND MARRIED-WOMAN SEX

You've been waiting to find out (maybe even skipped to this part of the book): What the heck are single-woman sex and married-woman sex, and what's the difference? Perhaps you're also fervently wishing, "Please, please, please let this be the two-minute-magic-bullet explanation so I don't have to read this entire book to get the answer." Yes, I will explain the difference, but sadly there is no magic bullet.

The premise to single-woman sex is deceptively simple, so please don't blink or you'll miss it. It's based on the idea that *men see sex as a means toward intimacy; while women see intimacy as a means toward sex.* The way we learn to have sex, that is single-women sex, is based in a "male" way of having sex (neither right nor wrong and certainly not a reason to point a finger of blame).

Single-woman sex is about getting each other "off," and after experiencing a wonderful orgasm, hoping those magnificent feelings will propel you to feel closer and more loving as a couple. This formula works well while we are in the throes of lust because there is plenty of built-in intimacy to satiate a woman's needs.

However, after a few years, problems arise when sex becomes compartmentalized in a couple's busy life. No energy, time and therefore letting sex coast, meant the once-easy-to-access intimacy gets disconnected. The sexual act that was once a multi-faceted experience becomes one-dimensional body mechanical sex and it ceases to meet most of her (and perhaps his) sexual needs.

The woman begins to collect a lot of negative what-have-you-done-for-me-lately feelings around the sexual experience. It's both of their individual negative feelings (unappreciated, frustrated, and resentful) and not the actual sexual act that translates into a big lack of desire. She's not enjoying the sexual experience and feels she's doing it for his benefit and in no way are her needs taken into consideration. So if the couple doesn't do anything to change their sexual dynamic, she begins to avoid sex because—drum roll please—single-woman sex makes her feel like she *has* to have sex. In sharp contrast, when a couple is able to keep a level of intimacy in and outside the bedroom, married-woman sex ensures she will *want* to have sex.

Come on, admit it, you're rolling your eyes, feeling let down, thinking, "Is that it? This is nothing new! A woman who feels intimately connected to her partner in and outside the bedroom is more likely interested in sex. Pulease." Okay, fine. But if we can get a bit philosophical, it's always the common-sense ideas that are the most difficult to work into your busy daily life—like eat healthy, exercise three times a week, take out a bit of "me time" every day to ensure balance.

Case in point: One popular myth is that successful sex means having the almighty orgasm. Now don't get me wrong, orgasms are pretty wonderful things; people sometimes go to great lengths to experience one. Unfortunately, with this belief firmly entrenched, it's one of the main reasons sex over the long term becomes dull. Has your current sex spun into the male way of having sex—sex is a means toward intimacy—he tries to get you off, he gets off, you go to the bathroom to de-goo and you're done? That fifteen minutes of ecstatic, mind-bending passion (yawn) is based on mechanical body, orgasm-focused sex, with little to no effort made to sexual finesse.

SEX IS A STATE OF MIND

The married-woman-sex formula of having good to amazing sex over the long term is a state of mind—or a woman's need for intimacy as a means toward sex. In observing any number of sexually successful couples, you will inevitably find one thing in common: a healthy, positive attitude toward their sex life. It doesn't mean they don't experience the same life challenges, disagreements, and ups and downs as you. They're real people. The simple difference is they frame their thinking around sex differently.

Just for an instant imagine your life exactly the way it is, but with sex being a welcome, integral part of your couple happiness. Voila, you've just experienced what these people live every day—the married-woman-sex dynamic.

It's just as certain, in observing sexually unhappy couples that they've developed negative feelings toward their sexual dynamic. And one of the big culprits that can lead you to sexual unhappiness is getting stuck in the rut of having single-woman sex: the focus on only "in, out, done" orgasm-driven sex.

Shalina's Story

To get a better sense of this negative sexual state of mind, here's an e-mail written from Shalina who miserably confessed: "I am 42 years old, had a baby three years ago, not overweight or depressed. But I have absolutely no sex drive. I wouldn't care if I went for the rest of my life without sex. I do have sex with my husband at least once a week for his benefit. He tries to get sex at least two or three times a week and I usually let him know I am just too tired. I get up at 5 a.m. every morning and get my three-year-old daughter ready for daycare. We are out the door by 6:20 a.m. every day. It is very stressful trying to get her ready. Then I commute to my job, work for 10 hours before commuting home 45 minutes. I arrive home at 6 p.m.

"So I think I am angry with my husband deep inside for asking for sex when I am so tired. I think of how selfish he can be thinking I am going to have sex for an hour starting at 10 p.m. when I have to get up in the morning. Plus, he never wants to have sex quickly. Whenever we have sex he feels the need to attend to my needs and keeps on attending to me until I have had multiple orgasms. I am happy with one and try to speed things up and move him along but I don't think he can get aroused until I have multiple orgasms. He never seems to be able to just have intercourse and skip the foreplay. Sometimes I am just not in the mood to spend so much time on me. I would be fine just having quick intercourse and then be done. So I avoid sex because it is so involved all the time.

"During most of our sexual encounters I am not faking the orgasms but I am thinking of other stuff during sex and thinking about how not into this I am and why can't he move it along. He has no idea I don't really enjoy our sex because I do have orgasms and tell him how great it was. Is it wrong to keep this up? I love him and don't want to make this an issue in our marriage. But I am miserable inside because I feel every time we get into bed or if I ask for a massage or some other touch, he turns it into sex. I have never had a big sex drive but it has diminished completely after the baby. What should I do?"

Can you relate to Shalina? She's fallen into the omnipresent single-woman-sex trap; she's able to orgasm and is fine with the bodily act, Rather, it's the negative state of mind that she has developed toward her sex life that's the problem: She feels put upon and cannot understand why he doesn't understand that sex is one more chore. Plus, Shalina's bought into the myth that sexual satisfaction equals orgasm.

Shalina needs to know that she is perfectly normal for not liking the way her sex life currently stands. Her life rushed ahead, while her sex stayed in her single-woman days. Shalina and her sex life must be harmonious with her present lifestyle—she needs to start having married-woman sex.

But first let's take a closer look at what comprises single-woman sex.

SINGLE-WOMAN SEX

Every person's sexuality is unique. The how, why, and what you believe about sex, and your sexual socialization, combines thousands of variables: your upbringing, education, where you lived, and friends, just to name a few. Everything you know and learned about sex over the years gives you a unique sexual fingerprint—and no two are the same. Yet, when you look at the average woman and how she figured out how to have sex, there are three main commonalities: clutching and grabbing the "hot spots," focusing on orgasm, and putting the man's needs before your own.

1. Clutching and Grabbing the "Hot Spots"

As we already discussed, your sexual socialization—how you learned to have sex—was pretty limited. How many teenagers learned sex in the back seat of their parents' car? (Lucky me, I got to experience a police officer shining his flashlight into the car, while my oblivious naked bottom was madly waving around for him to see). Lack of time, space, and youthful impatient hormones always had us frantic, propelling us to have hurry-up sex. It felt extremely good to touch, and be touched, on our "hot spots"—the three main sexual points, or erogenous zones on the body: breasts, vagina, and penis.

You learned men like to kiss and snuggle, but what they really, really love is oral sex and to have their penis rubbed. A guy learned that he has to kiss you (first base) for a long time before he could go for your breasts (second base). Then after enough time he can move onto your vulva area, with an extra bonus to you if he knows how to find your clitoris (third base). Finally once he's given you enough pleasure, maybe even an orgasm, he can move on to the main event, the grand finale of penis-vagina intercourse (home run). And let's not kid ourselves, in your young single days that clumsy groping and grasping of the hot spots was mind-blowing—and required minimal effort.

Here's the catch. Because you experienced a positive sexual rush from grabbing at the hot spots every single time, it became similar to a

Pavlovian response: you quickly started to associate really great feelings when your hot spots were being played with. In essence, you trained your brain that this was the only way to get a heady sexual blast. As a result, very early on you started associating only basic sex moves with what felt pleasurable and so formed an all-too-familiar sex pattern.

And hey, if it ain't broke, why fix it? In your single-woman-sex days, grabbing at your hot spots worked exceptionally well.

2. Focusing on Orgasm

Orgasms. So much of our focus has been given to that ten to fifteen seconds of body bliss.

Like everything else in our North American society, sex is goal driven. We have to have sex "X" times per week and each time we have sex we must achieve orgasm. There is an overwhelming perception that if we don't, we have failed sexually as a couple. Where did the notion of "successful sex equals an orgasm" come from?

The pioneers of sex research, like Sigmund Freud and Alfred Kinsey, created tangible, scientifically approved benchmarks for what was good or bad sex—not as easy as you might suspect. It makes sense that calculating orgasms was one of the few concrete measurements of sexual satisfaction. In the 1960s along came the famous sex research team of William Masters and Virginia E. Johnson, whose time in the laboratory coincided with the feminist movement. Why is this significant? A big agenda item for feminists was a woman's right to orgasm. Women who weren't able to achieve an orgasm made a mad scramble through the doors of Masters and Johnson's laboratory. Most of Masters and Johnson's findings therefore had to do with teaching women sexual satisfaction via orgasm.

Since then, this orgasm ideal has been studied, documented, and proven to be legitimate: couples who experience orgasms together tend to be more sexually satisfied than those who don't. I don't disagree with this theory, but it has created a skewed sensibility around the average couple's sex life.

You likely learned that a sexually satisfied couple will consistently orgasm with every sexual encounter. If we follow this logic, the more orgasms you have, the more sexually satisfied you should be. But as we saw with Shalina, she experienced multiple orgasms with every sexual encounter and was in no way sexually satisfied.

You see, an orgasm is multidimensional—physical, physiological, mental, spiritual. Single-woman sex has couples focusing on only the physical aspect, resulting in a one-dimensional experience. Only ever having single-woman sex drops the other equally important reasons an orgasm is so special. Couples need to feel the whole deal when experiencing this wonder.

This gets more messy if your guy believes that once you reach orgasm, you're sexually satisfied. What he doesn't know because (sigh) most of us women don't tell him, is that your body can experience an orgasm without you being sexually aroused, satisfied, or happy with the sexual experience. You might even fake excitement or orgasm just to get the sex over with.

Therefore, there has to be more to satisfying sex than simply experiencing an orgasm, particularly in a longer-term relationship.

3. Putting His Needs before Yours

The most basic, instinctual reason human beings have sexual intercourse is to procreate. For procreation to take place, a man must ejaculate his semen into a woman's vagina. If all goes well, in nine months a baby will come along, ensuring the couple's lineage and the survival of the human species. It makes sense then, that men and women have intuited throughout recent history, that in order for sex to be successful, the man must orgasm.

Before the 1960s feminist movement, men and women understood their sexual lot in life. Women saw sex as their "wifely duty"; it was a bonus if she enjoyed sex and if not she simply "stared at the ceiling and thought of England." The concept of women being equal in the bedroom and having as much right to sexual enjoyment has been around for fewer than fifty years. As much as both men and women would *love* to have women equal and active participants in bedroom goings-on, women are still playing catch-up to the notion of sexual emancipation.

This is usually where men get their boxers in a right twist, vehemently proclaiming that satisfying her needs always come before satisfying their own. I would wholeheartedly agree the average North American man considers his partner's sexual satisfaction a duty and that he is more than happy to oblige.

Here's the rub: In the first two years of your relationship when he massaged your breasts and clitoris, gave a bit of oral sex, you probably had a wonderful orgasm experience. He learned, and both of you came to understand, that once you orgasmed, you were adequately and sexually satisfied.

Fast-forward a couple more years: when the sex starts, he immediately goes to give you an orgasm; however, although you enjoy orgasms, they no longer meet all of your sexual expectations. Sex is no longer on your terms and unfortunately, this is where a couple's long-term sex challenge slides into: If your man can give you a fantastic orgasm, he's a stud. If he doesn't, oh well. But no matter what happens he must perform the big orgasmic finale for both of you to feel like the sex is complete and successful.

The Single-Woman Sex Formula

When we're single, this single-woman sex formula worked because going for the hot spots brings the maximum pleasure for minimum effort. Having an orgasm is, well, quite simply fantastic. And for him doing his best to make you orgasm proves he's a good guy. Therefore single-woman sex is fabulous when a relationship is in its infancy.

For too many women, however, the single-woman-sex formula stops working over the long haul. Unlike our pre-1960s female counterparts, women now expect at least a little sexual satisfaction from the experience. Yet, when single-woman sex goes unchecked, sex is no longer the fulfilling experience it used to be and she resents getting nothing out of the sex. Consciously or unconsciously, she feels he's gotten his way, again, and falls asleep having at least some fun while she gets zip, zilch, nada. Her sexual needs have come second again; it's not fair and she's not happy. It's terribly frustrating for both of them that she doesn't know why she's not satisfied—and therefore can't tell him. When it happens too many times, the sexual experience goes from fab, to not so great, to complete avoidance on her part.

Let's take a look at the cumulative effects of single-woman sex. That is, when the sensual side of sex doesn't happen, sex turns into one more chore.

YOUR NEGATIVE EMOTIONS TOWARD SEX

You're happy enough with your partner. Besides a few disagreements and the inevitable times when you just don't get each other, your relationship is pretty stable. Sex isn't what it used to be, but neither of you know for certain how to manage it, so it doesn't get discussed. But it creates a lot of tension. Chances are, if the tension goes unchecked, one day you wake up with a lot of "unexplained," unexpressed anger.

To better understand, let's look at your post-honeymoon relationship. The following is a typical example, although your relationship probably has its own variations.

Is Today the Day You Have to Have Sex?

You come home after a bone-weary long day. You, hopefully with your partner's help, throw a meal together, feed, wash, and put the kids to bed and do the housework you simply can't ignore. By this time it's getting late, and you're tired. You sink into the couch to veg for a precious hour before bedtime.

Out of the blue, your partner gives you his "let's have sex" look, or starts the oh-too-familiar pawing at your shoulders/breasts/butt, making it quite clear he wants to get a little action tonight. Your face discreetly settles into the "You're joking, right?" expression. From head to toe your body automatically seizes up; a sharp intake of breath, alarms going off all over the place. Sex tonight? Come on! Could he be a bigger, more selfish buffoon? Can't he see I'm exhausted? A little peace and quiet is the only thing I want a piece of tonight. Yet you realize it's been a while since your last sexual escapade.

You Become a Victim to Your Sex

He has initiated sex but you don't feel like it. Just as likely you feel guilty about it. Guilt nags at you that it's been a week (or two or three) since the last time you've had sex and that statistic will stand, plaguing you, until you actually do something. You reason that you don't really feel like having sex when you're feeling guilty, but you sort of have to, since it's been so long. It seems so unfair. Why does he always get his way?

Guilt reminds you it's not your guy's fault. He's a good man and deserves to get some. Plus if you don't do it now, it might cause a fight—and you really, really don't want to start yet another disagreement around sex. Resentfully, you drag yourself to the bedroom.

Whereas many men seem to have an on-off switch to snap into the mood, you haven't had a chance to properly process your day, and your multi-tasking brain is still locked on information overload. There is a tiny awkward pause where both of you don't know how or where to start. Then like clockwork, your clothes come off (seductively peeling each other's clothes off, and having candles, wine, and soft music no longer happens). You both start the old familiar sex dance. He understands he must "sexually satisfy" you first by giving you an orgasm. To turn your engines over, he does what he was taught worked during your first few years together: fondling your hot spots.

Alas, his hard work is doing nothing for you. Instead of feeling good, it's quite simply an overload to your worn-out senses. You want to tell him to stop, slow down, or at the very least take it easy, but you don't want to hurt his feelings and get into a disagreement. You wish you could tell him the sex rules to your sexual satisfaction have changed, but, heck, you probably don't know them yourself.

As his advances become just too much, you either squirm away from his touch or you let him bring you to orgasm because he just won't quit until you've reached that point. Even if you've experienced an orgasm, your body maybe neither be sufficiently excited nor even lubricated.

Now that you've orgasmed, faked it, or at least indicated it's not going to happen for you tonight, your turn for sexual enjoyment is over (for which you're most grateful). Your mission is to get his orgasm over and done with. And so it's on to the main event. The intercourse that follows is all about you being instrumental to create the "get-on, get-in, get-off, now go to sleep" type of sex.

You both automatically assume the first intercourse position. As he gets closer to climax, he flips you into the second sexual position, which most likely is doggie style to get the best penetration. At this point, unless you're able to have a vaginal orgasm—and only about 33 per cent of women can do so consistently (see Appendix 1 for more information)—the penetration feels all right, but deep down you hope the thrusting doesn't last for more than five minutes. You go along for the ride, helping him get it over with more quickly. You can feel his body tense, hear his, "I'm just about ready to cum" grunts and groans. *Finally*, he ejaculates.

You go to the bathroom to de-goo yourself, come back to bed, and wonder if his now-sleeping gooey naked body will mess up your freshly cleaned sheets. (Which reminds you, why can't he do the laundry for once?) The sex? Well, the sex seemed satisfying for him, but a waste of time for you. But you would never admit that to him because you would feel terrible and it would probably start a disagreement. (Gosh, are we starting to see a pattern of you avoiding a fight at the cost of your sexual satisfaction ... hmmm ... very interesting.)

Resentment Comes Next

At this point, guilt is replaced by resentment. As you're lying there sexually unsatisfied, resentment reminds you that this is the way sex has been for quite some time. You feel helpless and start blaming your guy for your lack of sexual happiness. Why is it so easy for him to put his sexual needs first? Doesn't he get it? Can't he see how exhausted you are? Here you are working like a madwoman trying to juggle a job, home, and kids—he comes to bed wanting a piece of you too. You start to feel like you're simply an instrument for his sexual pleasure.

Resentment convinces you it doesn't matter that you haven't had a productive discussion around sex and he is in the dark about your sexual unhappiness. Resentment reminds you that he should at the very least be able to read your body language and know that sex isn't what you want it to be. You forget that men need a straightforward conversation about sex and your sex life. Your hinting, eye rolling, and being a less-enthusiastic bed partner is simply going to make him frustrated. Resentment feeds your belief that when it comes to sex, your partner should be the one who initiates a warm, caring heart-to-heart conversation.

Are You at the Apathetic Stage?

When you've gone through this destructive sex cycle enough times, it's easy to take your victimization to the next level and become apathetic. Besides the "groping" approach to sex being part of the problem, resentment from other parts of your life, the many demands put upon you, and the pressure to do everything well becomes overwhelming. Once you're apathetic, enjoying sex becomes much harder because you just stop caring; you don't feel guilt or resentment—you just don't care. Soon enough, sex becomes something you actively avoid.

Perpetuating the Negative Sex Cycle

Floundering with how to make sex work, you might have reached the apathetic point in your relationship. To try to understand, you seek a reason for your lagging sex desire. Perhaps you've bought into pop culture's mantras: your busy lifestyle is the cause of your lack of libido; having kids automatically means you put your sex life on the back burner for the next eighteen years; once the marriage starts, the sex ends.

Frantic, you go on the Internet and research how you've "lost" your libido. One website suggests you may have a hormone imbalance. A magazine article you came across points out that the two of you need to communicate better. So you initiate ways to communicate better and it works—for about a week.

Not yet defeated, you go to the bookstore, and tentatively slink down the sex aisle. There you find multiple books on sexual techniques and sexual positions. With high hopes, you take the books home; though both of you are titillated, nothing changes. You are still left unsatisfied with every sexual encounter.

At this point you find yourself right back at square one, none the wiser, except with a bigger feeling of apathy. You're desperate, but too ashamed to speak to a therapist. You're stuck in a negative sex rut induced by having only single-woman sex. To recap:

1. You love your partner.
2. You do want to have sex and find it enjoyable but only when you're in the mood.
3. Although you can orgasm, sex isn't as satisfying as it once was.
4. Your life has fundamentally changed in every way and yet your sex has stayed the (yawn) same.

There Is a Solution to Your Woes

The real and best solution for this situation is to jump on the married-woman-sex bandwagon. And quick. But first a word of caution: before you get all zany, going to the back of this book to immediately implement the married-woman sex techniques, you need to pull the single-woman-sex weeds out of your garden before the beautiful married-woman-sex flowers can grow.

You have to change how you feel about sex, yourself, your body, and how you feel about having sex with your partner.

MARRIED-WOMAN SEX

So far, we've talked extensively about what married-woman sex is not. So here is a brief explanation of what married-woman sex is. Don't worry, there'll be more. In fact the rest of this book is dedicated to helping you create this positive sexual dynamic. Married-woman sex means you make yourself an equal in the bedroom; your body is your sexual ally, and you create a sex life that is both fun and meaningful and on your terms.

1. You Make Yourself an Equal in the Bedroom

Today's women have grown up being told they are equal in every way. Indeed, when the birth control pill burst on the scene in the 1960s, it put women's sexual equality on the map. While it is true sexual progress was evident in your single-woman sex, sadly not much has changed from your grandmother's era in terms of long-term sex.

Intellectually you probably understand that your sexual needs are just as important as his, but your follow-through on this feminist principle might be a little weak. For too many women, there is a huge gap between how you're supposed to be, feel, and act in the bedroom and what actually occurs. Unbeknownst to both of you, unspoken equality expectations hang over your sex life; that initiation, sexual appetite, sexual adventurousness, and so on must be mutually shared and equal—which is rarely the case.

When you don't ask for what you want, your needs are not met and it becomes a source of guilt, anxiety, and depression.

Therefore, the first step into married-woman sex—your sexual equality— is knowing what you want your sex life to be and what satisfying sex means to you. Currently, satisfying your sexual needs usually means him giving you an orgasm before he can have his turn. But if this doesn't do the trick, you must figure out what does. It's perfectly acceptable if what you consider to be good sex is different from what your partner believes is good sex. If you truly are in fact an equal in the bedroom, what you want is as important as what he wants.

Most likely what you want out of the sexual experience is to feel nurtured and have positive and constant intimacy or connection with your partner. More importantly, what you want will almost certainly not follow society's prescribed rules on what constitutes a successful sex life—that sexually successful couples mechanically have sex "X" times per week and orgasms with every sexual encounter. In fact, for you, having sexual intercourse may become a secondary aspect to your day-to-day lovemaking enjoyment.

Sexual equality also means speaking your piece; being able to confidently say, "I only want to have foreplay tonight and not intercourse" or "Please move it over to the left, you're not hitting the spot" or "You're thrusting a little too hard for my poor little cervix," or "I know you want to have sex eighteen times per week, but we're going to have to make it once every couple of weeks for the next few months work."

Sexual equality means that if your sexual needs have not been met, and he's already had his orgasm, sex will continue until you're both mutually satisfied.

2. Your Body is Your Sexual Ally

Most women numb themselves from their necks down and set up permanent residence in their multi-tasking brains. Although your body gives you cues and clues all the time, because you don't pay attention it is difficult to be aware of your unique sexual rhythm. Married-woman sex will have you paying attention to your body and its signs.

You need to discover how your body, at different points of your menstrual cycle, wants intense or mellow lovemaking. To feel naked-body confident so you can shake what your momma gave you. Knowing the difference between sexual arousal, desire, and libido can have a dramatic impact on your experience. Arousal comprises the physical signs that show you are turned on; desire comprises the thoughts you have toward the act of sex; and libido comprises what drives you to have sex. Good sex means you need to get back in touch with your body—if you were ever in touch in the first place.

3. You Create a Sex Life That is Both Fun and Meaningful and on Your Terms

Presently, what is perceived to satisfy a woman's sexual needs and create her sex drive is measured by a male standard of sexual satisfaction. As a result, the all-important intimacy and non-demand pleasuring are sacrificed because emphasis is too much placed on the act of intercourse. Your sexual satisfaction depends on sex being as much about outer course as it is about intercourse.

Creating sex on your terms requires a paradigm shift in your thinking: from you being passive about sex to being proactive about your sex life. It's you taking charge (at least once in a while) in the bedroom. No longer waiting for your guy to say what and when you're going to do when having sex. Once you make the shift in your thinking, sex becomes welcome instead of another to-do on your chore list.

Implementing married-woman sex into your relationship—being an equal, being in touch with your body, and having sex on your terms—are easily achievable. The key is to take baby steps.

It's Time to Put Theory into Action

Being a busy woman and creating a satisfying sex life doesn't have to be an arduous, soul-searching journey. It does mean work—but nothing you can't manage. Yes, you'll have to give up your victim baggage and rework your domestic routine a bit. You'll also have to figure out how you want sex to be and implement positive changes. But these are small potatoes when they result in a life filled with fun and meaningful sex.

The rest of the book will help you take small steps to achieve your goal. If you're still feeling a bit overwhelmed about the impending change, compare the difference in expending your energy to put your sex life back on track to choosing to do nothing. In their book *Rekindling Desire*, Barry and Emily McCarthy say it best, "The adage in sex therapy is that when sexuality goes well, it is a positive, integral but not a major component—adding 15 to 20 per cent to the marital vitality and satisfaction. However, when sexuality is dysfunctional or nonexistent, it assumes an inordinately powerful role, 50 to 70 per cent, robbing the marriage of intimacy and vitality."

Isn't it just a teeny bit exciting to think that, just around the corner, there is a new, better, shiny sex life waiting for you? No longer do you have to put up with the base model of sex, when you can have all the bells and whistles. And the really cool thing is that you're the driver.

DO YOU NEED THIS BOOK OR COUNSELLING?

Kudos to you. Understanding that your sexual relationship isn't going the way you would like it to and deciding to do something about it is a huge step.

I hope that reading this book helps you see your sexual relationship differently. I truly believe that a book or a quote, a paragraph, or an example, can give you that sudden leap of understanding to help you turn your thinking around and make the needed changes in your life.

Sometimes though, marital issues—which intertwine themselves with and are almost indistinguishable from personal issues—run deep and are too complicated for people to sort through themselves. Granted, fixing things yourself works to a certain extent; however, your level of objectivity is limited. Trying to untangle the issues you and your partner have built up can be, quite simply, overwhelming.

With everything else going on with your life, you might feel it easier to toss this book aside, do nothing, and ignore what's happening in your relationship. Don't do it!

Seeing a counsellor, therapist, or religious adviser can be a win-win proposition. These trained professionals, objective third parties, make their livelihood from helping people improve their lives. Your chances of working through difficult issues and moving forward in a happy relationship dramatically increase.

Unfortunately, seeing a therapist is often viewed as a weakness. I'm unsure why counsellors have such a bad rap. Sure, some people believe that you should just suck it up, never show your vulnerabilities, not air your "dirty laundry," and certainly not ask for help. I think that's complete hogwash. In my opinion, it's the smart people who seek help.

Elite Athletes Do It

Think about elite athletes. These people were born with, and over a lifetime perfect, their athletic gift. You would think these, of all people, wouldn't need someone helping them practise *every day*. And yet, accompanying every step of an athlete's journey is a coach. Coaches are especially needed when their athlete hits a slump. Together they work extra hard to get out of the slump and back to being their best.

Getting a "coach" to help you out of your slump will help get you, your marriage, and your sexuality back to peak performance. The bonus: you'll get back on track in a fraction of the time and with less frustration than it would take you to sort through all the issues on your own.

Your Partner Doesn't Want To

Maybe you're concerned that your partner doesn't want to have anything to do with a therapist. Have you brought up the topic? Better yet, have you two been able to lovingly and supportively discuss seeing a therapist? When faced with change or grappling with a huge negative situation, most people's first reaction will be to say no. If your partner refuses to go, then go alone.

When your partner sees your progress, he might agree to join you. If he digs in his heels and refuses, keep going. That's the point of the book: Focus on what you want your sexual relationship to be instead of what it currently is. Seeing a counselor might be *your* best option, whether your partner agrees with that option or not.

If you don't know where to look for a qualified therapist, check the Resources on page 214. You'll be happy you took the therapist step.

KEY POINTS

1. Don't fret if your once-fabulous sex turned into something you now actively avoid. There's a perfectly logical reason.

2. Romantic love sets up an unrealistic expectation about how your long-term sex life should be.

3. Long-term sex gets boring after only a few years because you keep having the same old single-woman sex. Single-woman sex is about grabbing the "hot spots," focuses on orgasm, and puts the man's needs first.

4. As the relationship evolves and the sex does not, a lot of tension is created until one day the couple wakes up with a lot of unexpressed anger.

5. Married-woman sex has the woman making herself an equal; uses her body's natural sexual rhythm to her advantage on her terms; and is a positive, self-affirming, and integrated space that easily fits into the context of her busy life.

6. This book can help you in many ways; however, you need to determine is your relationship simply needs a sexual tune-up or if you need to talk to a professional to work through deeper issues.

CHAPTER 2

Getting Real with Your Single-Woman-Sex Situation

"I didn't always like him and he didn't always like me. The thing is I always came back to why I married him in the first place and it seemed to get me through those not so great times."

—Bea Bell, married fifty-two years with three children

IT'S PERFECTLY NORMAL NOT TO LIKE SEX AFTER MARRIAGE; HOWEVER ...

Okay, so now you understand that what's happened to your sex life is status quo for millions of couples. Isn't it a relief to know you aren't some kind of freak—or at least if you are, everyone else is a freak too? If you stopped reading the book here, just knowing that would have been worth your effort.

The next two chapters—fortunately or unfortunately depending on how you look at it—are about you courageously walking into your sex closet and sorting all the dirty laundry. Like most women, you've probably pushed all the negative feelings associated with your sex life—

guilt, resentment, and apathy—to the side just to get through your busy days. Ignoring, denying, and being comfortably numb with your state of sex is probably far more appealing than opening a can of worms. However, it's best to get all the crummy stuff out of the way while you're still motivated and excited about making changes to your sex life.

To start, let's look at the five stages of a relationship then take an honest look at which stage your relationship is in. This assessment will become the baseline of your sexual-happiness measuring stick and will be a good indication of just how much work will be necessary to turn your situation around.

Stage 1: You've Met the Perfect Partner

Typically in Stage 1 you feel incredibly lucky to have this person in your life. The tender trap of romantic love clouds your judgment, has you walking into walls, and makes your privates ache because you want to have sex so badly. In the first six months to two years of your relationship, you feel, act like, and understand that you've met the perfect partner. You're sexually self-confident; able to be open, vulnerable, and transparent; and your libido is fuelled by all the "love drugs" coursing through your veins. Raunchy sex is effortless. Everything is lovey-dovey, rose-coloured, and, sunshiny perfect. Throughout the years together couples will experience short periods of this bliss.

Stage 2: You Look for and Find Everything Wrong with Your Partner

Here, relationship reality strikes and your once-perfect partner has started turning into a bit of a jerk. His fall from grace is harsh—for both of you. But, really, it's quite natural when you live, eat, and sleep in such close proximity to someone (anyone) that they will, without exception, begin to grate on your nerves. Every person has minor and major character flaws. In this stage the flaws become more noticeable and you can't help but want to "help" your partner fix them.

Stage 3: Instead of Blaming your Partner, You Look Inward and Begin Making Changes in Yourself

The very act of buying this book says that you are most likely moving into Stage 3 (or, at least, want to be). So give yourself a pat on the back! Bravo. Well done for boldly stepping into Stage 3. You no longer want to be a victim to your sexual circumstance and have decided to take responsibility and do something about your part in the sexual equation. You've realized you cannot change your partner; you can change only yourself. By working on yourself and your issues and making changes to how you perceive your sex life, you will see your sex life turn around.

Stage 4: You and Your Partner Become Friends

After you've both worked through some of your personal issues, and taken responsibility for why this relationship has become they way it has, it's time to move into the next phase—becoming friends again. The fog has lifted and you can see why you got together with your partner in the first place. Make sure you throw a big party after you make it out of Stage 3 and into Stage 4. You deserve a big celebration for all of your hard work and effort. At the very least, acknowledge and cherish this time.

Side note: At the time of writing this book, my husband and I are in Stage 4. Although it feels great to be each other's friends again, we both can see how fragile this stage is and how easily we could be knocked off course. Please know that just because we're here doesn't mean there are fewer days of frustration and disagreements (I wish). The relationship is what we had before we started all of this. However, now we are working to keep our relationship in our top three priorities—no longer allowing our relationship to coast. Our efforts are making all the difference to keeping our intimate connection alive and well.

Stage 5: You Enter into the Bliss Part of the Relationship

This is the holy grail of sticking it out with one person for thirty-plus years—the proverbial cherry on life's sundae. Have you ever seen a couple in their eighties, holding hands, heads together, talking as if they were the only two people in existence? It's what so many of us long for and dream to have in our relationship. To have the incredible connection and friendship that can come only after many, many years of successfully making it through life's ups and downs.

ASSESS YOUR RELATIONSHIP STAGE

At what stage would you place your sexual relationship? Many couples who keep having single-woman sex get caught at Stage 2. They're so busy blaming each other for why sex doesn't work that they never take the time to point the finger at themselves. So here are the ground rules for moving into Stage 3.

It's Time for Some Straight Talk

The paradox about Stage 2 (when you look for and find everything wrong with your partner) is that it isn't your partner's idiosyncrasies that are making you crazy; rather, it's your own insecurities you are battling. What you find "wrong" with your partner—such as irritating personal habits, unfair division of household and child care tasks—most likely is what you're not willing, wanting, or ready to take on yourself.

You may wonder how self-esteem could be connected, for example, when your husband's job which has him travelling and leaving you with all the household responsibilties? Chances are it comes down to an inability or an insecurity to assertively communicate your needs, wants, and desires. If you were able to negotiate that what you needed from this relationship was more help with the house and kids to make you happy, you wouldn't be feeling resentful.

Therefore, when you refuse to deal with your self-esteem issues, and they rear their ugly heads, you project them onto someone else. And the easiest person upon whom to foist your issues and insecurities is the person closest to you: your partner. Usually the more fault you find with your partner, the lower your own self-esteem. This is also true when he finds fault with you.

The end result? Most people automatically default to a victim stance during minor or major life upheavals. This means you don't take responsibility for how your insecurities (and the way you project them on to your partner) are contributing to your unhappiness as a couple. When you don't take responsibility, you cannot resolve the problem and fix your circumstance. Low self-esteem does not a sex kitten make.

Moving from Stage 2 to Stage 3 might mean taking responsibility and initiating change by yourself. Many women ask, why should they do all the work while their guy sits back and reaps the benefits? For right now, you'll just have to trust that once you get this ball rolling, he will be on board. But first here are some things to think about.

If You Don't Like Each Other, Why Are You Trying to Have Sex?

You must also keep your focus forward; that is always keep in mind what you want out of this relationship. Having good sex means you have to (1) like sex and (2) like the person with whom you're having sex. Playing games with each others' feelings (e.g., put-downs, always being angry) shows externally that you don't like each other much. However, while sabotaging their partner, couples still expect to have mind-blowing sex. Huh? Why would you want to have sex with someone who has just completely ticked you off? Stay focused on how your partner is trying to change and help the process along— although at times it might not seem apparent.

Let Go of Any Control-Freak Tendencies

If you're a control freak, like me, and need things to go exactly as expected, you need to change that. You need to be flexible with change and be okay if he doesn't want to do things your way.

You see, your personal issues and insecurities will be different from your partner's. So when you map out the best possible route to put your sex back on track, your logic will be based on battling your particular issues. Your partner has his own set of issues and will therefore come up a different route. You're both right. It's okay if your paths to resolution go in separate directions as long as you both have the same goal in mind: to be closer, more intimate, and enjoy sex.

What If He Is Less Than Receptive?

Have faith, once you get the ball rolling, your partner will want to come along on the ride. If at first you're making grandiose efforts and he's doing nothing, realize that it takes time for any human being to make changes that weren't their idea in the first place.

What If He's Being a Downright Jerk?

In the worst-case (and least likely) scenario, your partner will dig in his heels and refuse to move out of Stage 2. He won't acknowledge what you are doing, or he may even try to sabotage your great efforts. He's most likely scared. Ordinary change is scary enough; changing things around sex is in another league. Don't worry about why he is behaving in such a manner. Don't back down or give up your efforts. Simply do your best to push forward and create a new dynamic.

In order to make it to Stage 4, being friends, and then hopefully on to Stage 5, that heavenly bliss, you must take a brave leap of faith. Move yourselves out of Stage 2 and into Stage 3.

Let's look at some ways to help you make the move.

YOUR SEX SNAPSHOT: THEN AND NOW

The amount of time, effort, and energy you put into anything is what you get back from that experience. You need to figure out how your positive, negative, or neutral energy has created your sexual dynamic.

Energy Equals Quality of Sex

Time spent = What you prioritize = Where you put your energy
Positive energy = Positive sex experience

The next time you wake up in a great mood, pay close attention to how it impacts everyone around you. Positive energy results in positive feelings; positive feelings bring about positive thoughts; positive thoughts cause positive actions; positive actions produce positive feelings, and the cycle continues. The same is true for negative thoughts and for neutral thoughts.

Consequently, it's no surprise you had amazing sex in the first couple of years: there was an abundance of positive couple energy. You were both lust struck and neither of you could do any wrong. As you frantically tried to impress your new heartthrob, he responded with the same warm fuzzy feelings. Your positive couple energy radiated and made everyone around you feel incredibly special. In fact, between the two of you, your positive sexual energy could have lit up an entire city.

How has that energy exchange changed over your years together? I would venture you have set your couple energy on cruise control, with little or no effort to make each other and sex a priority on a daily basis. I suppose it's better than fighting; however, putting no effort into your relationship is creating your blah sex results. And if you're stuck in Stage 2, always looking for and finding everything wrong with your partner, you can sometimes get caught up in a destructive negative-energy loop. *Good sex cannot thrive when it's being fed negative energy.*

Now that you've figured out at which stage your relationship stands, it's time to measure the amount of positive, negative, or neutral energy you currently infuse into it. How do you do this? By taking a before-and-after snapshot of the time, effort, and energy you put into your relationship.

Snapshot of Your "Before" Efforts

Here are the top ten qualities of positive couple energy you experienced at the start of your relationship.

1. **You laughed and smiled a lot:** Simply thinking, being around, or mentioning your partner's name put a big smile on your face.

2. **The "fuss" factor:** You primped and preened, making sure you looked freshly scrubbed and presentable for your partner. It was all those little things, like dabbing on perfume, plucking your eyebrows, looking twice in the mirror to make sure you looked your best.

3. **You spoke about your partner in positive terms:** You couldn't wait to gush about this person to anyone who was willing to listen—how wonderful he was and how you two were a perfect fit. You couldn't believe that this person had come into your life.

4. **You daydreamed about a bright, hopeful future:** Come on, admit it, in the first few weeks together visions of wedding dresses and silver patterns danced through your head.

5. **You were interested in what your partner told you:** You hung on his every word. Talking for hours about any topic was effortless. Conversations were lively and fun.

6. **You initiated fun:** Being together was all about creating a good time. You put a lot of thought into fun activities the two of you could experience—going on picnics, leaving love notes, taking off for the weekend on a moment's notice, or making special dinners when you did stay in.

7. **Touch was electric:** Do you remember the first time you two touched? Your skin was on fire, and when you were apart you craved the next time you would be able to touch again. It was all about being up close and personal, often finding yourself wrapped around him like a pretzel.

8. **You created a sexy atmosphere:** You wanted sex time between the two of you to be special. Candles, bubble baths, and everything sensual was always at your fingertips. In fact, you probably spent a lot of time in bed, not necessarily getting down and dirty, but simply hanging out and touching each other.

9. **You had a sense of sexual adventure:** Sex was new, exciting, and fun, giving you a surge of sexual self-confidence. You were able to go outside your comfort zone and try, maybe even

suggest, adventurous things. You were open to learning new tips and tricks from each other to make sex all the more fun.

10. **You wanted to show off your sexual prowess:** Fuelled by your newfound sexual self-confidence, you wanted to prove to this person that you knew what you were doing in the sack. You might have even won an award for your sex-kitten performances—porn stars had nothing on you.

Can you see how your once-good energy created your once-great sex? Having good sex was easy at the start because you put a lot of good energy into it.

Snapshot of Your "After" Efforts

Now it's time to get real and find out how much energy you put into making your couple time special. How often do you:

1. Laugh and smile when you're together?
2. Fuss about looking good especially for him?
3. Talk to other people about how wonderful your partner is?
4. Daydream about your happy sexy future?
5. Are keenly interested in what your partner is doing or telling you about?
6. Initiate fun for you two?
7. Touch him sensually?
8. Create a sexy atmosphere?
9. Try something new or sexually adventurous?
10. Show him your wild side?

Another way of looking at this would be if you were to go on a date today, what would it look like?

Now compare your "before" and "after" lists. Chances are that your "before" list shows that you put in a lot more positive energy at the beginning of your relationship.

If you were rating your partner and feel strongly that the quality of your relationship has changed because of his actions, perhaps this would be a good starting point for a *constructive* conversation.

Energy Is Created from What You Value

You're busy. I get it.

Please don't think I'm suggesting it's realistic for you to spend every ounce of your energy creating a constant, pulsating stream of sexy energy like you did when you first got together. Yet, it's important to take a look at what you prioritize because what you prioritize is where you'll put your energy. A small (and overused example) of how couples expend their energy would be this: The average North American couple spends a minimum twenty hours per week watching TV and only about fifteen to twenty minutes every week on their sex.

Giving up TV time for ten minutes a day is an adjustment to your routine that will turn into wonderful couple energy. It means a shift in your routine and a shift in your values (both of which we will be covering). Putting energy back into your sex life doesn't have to be arduous or complicated; it is as simple as ten minutes per day. Ten minutes a day means over an hour per week, about five hours per month, sixty hours per year. This small change in how you divide your energy and time will have a drastic effect on your sex life.

HOT, STEAMY SEX IN YOUR COMFY SWEATPANTS?

One of the first places couples stop making efforts is in their appearance. Although it really is what's on the inside that counts, looking good for partners tends to go down the drain once you know they've been caught. No energy put into how you look means you probably don't feel sexy.

It should be in wedding vows alongside love, honour, and cherish that from this day forward the neon-green sweatpants or the fraying-elastic period-panties *are* allowed to surface into everyday wear. When you get home after a hard day, it's only to be expected you immediately take off your bra, makeup, and work clothes; let down your guard; and get comfortable. It is, for all intents and purposes, a rite of relationship passage.

However, a key element to great sex is to always have a sense of the erotic—the desire to feel pleasure. Erotic feelings are based on your expectations of romantic love. Romantic love, as we already discussed, is built on instability and the unknown. Unfortunately, everything comfortable about your relationship can be poisonous to sexual novelty and excitement.

Domestic routine equals you taking a low-sex-drive pill every morning. Plus the more committed you are to your domestic routine (like when you have small children) the harder it may be for you to put on your sexy party pants and have a fun time in bed.

In her book, *Mating in Captivity*, Esther Perel aptly wrote:

> You meet someone through a potent alchemy of attraction. It is a sweet reaction and it's always a surprise. You're filled with a sense of possibility, of hope, of being lifted out of the mundane and into a world of emotion and enthrallment. Love grabs you, and you feel powerful. You cherish the rush, and you want to hold on to the feeling. You're also scared. The more you become attached, the more you have to lose. So you set out to make love more secure. You seek to fix it, to make it dependable. You make your first commitments, and happily give up a little bit of freedom in exchange for a little bit of stability. You create comfort through devices—habit, ritual, pet names—that bring reassurance. But the excitement was bound to a certain measure of insecurity. Your high resulted from insecurity, and now, by seeking to harness it, you wind up draining the vitality out of the relationship. You enjoy comfort, but complain that you feel constrained. You miss spontaneity. In your attempt to control the risks of passion, you have tamed it out of existence. Marital boredom is born.

What's a Couple to Do?

When erotica meets I-no-longer-have-to-shave-my-legs domestic bliss, it's like two forces repelling each other. The general population wants to feel safe by having everyone conform to a specific set of life rules. As such, there's a tremendous expectation put on long-term couples to settle down and create a stable life.

Inside a brand-new relationship, you lay the groundwork for what will become the rest of your life's routine: buy a house; have a few disagreements; figure out who gets to take the first shower, if the television is on during the morning, whether talking is strictly forbidden before the first cup of coffee. You have a couple of years alone then you must look seriously at having kids.

Once you've ticked marriage, a mortgage and kids off your to-do list, it is your job to be a good solid citizen; work hard; have a beautiful and well-kept home; and raise well-behaved children who will be good citizens and contribute to society. All very honourable things to be sure, but the harder you strive for these ideals, the more you move away from cultivating your erotic desire. After you get into a long-term relationship, your time—and therefore lack of sexual choice—belongs to your kids, your boss, your extended family. Pretty much everyone but you.

Your Typical Anti-Erotic Day

When you take a look at your daily grind, there's little mystery why sex is no longer a pulsating throb between your legs, impatiently waiting to be satisfied. Does your week look something like this? Monday morning, your alarm goes off and, if possible, you hit the snooze button several times. You get up, drag your butt out of bed, go start a pot of coffee, then take a shower before the bathroom gets full of steam and questionable smells. Commute to work. Deal with office politics. Come home, make supper, and wash up. Do some light housecleaning. Have an hour or so to "relax." Go to bed semi-exhausted.

When kids come along, the need to get into a deeper routine is mandatory. Gone are the days of going out at a moment's notice— not that you ever did but at least you had the opportunity. For the sanity of you and your child(ren) it's all about disciplined routine, routine, routine. Get the kids up. Get them ready. Send them off to school. Cook breakfast, lunch, snacks, and supper. Take the kids to soccer practice, Scouts or Guides, tap dance lessons, or whatever extracurricular activities they're involved in. Supervise homework. Put the kids to bed. Then do some light housecleaning. Try to relax. Go to bed semi-exhausted.

Repeat routine Tuesday, Wednesday, Thursday, and Friday. Saturday go grocery shopping and run all the other errands that you couldn't get done during the workweek. Sunday, you have a tiny precious bit of time to relax. Starting mid-afternoon you ramp up to the next week. Do over again, and again, and again until your brain goes semi-numb.

Does reading this make you feel hot, bothered, and sexy all over like the first time you got together with your mate? The minutiae of your daily routine are not exactly a breeding ground for hot, tumultuous blow-your-head-off sex. In fact, I'm in awe that busy couples have sex at all.

Vacation Sex

When you get out of the daily grind and into a new routine, it's amazing how your sexual desire comes around. I've had a number of women ask why, when on vacation, having sex becomes easier, even (gasp!) fun. Part of it is not having the pressure of kids, cellphone, e-mail, or housework (thank goodness for hotels). The other part is you're temporarily removed from your usual dull routine. This change of scenery gives your erotic sexual desire a wake-up shake and puts sex back on the map.

Rebecca confessed to me that for at least a year her sex life had hit rock bottom. Then due to some house damage, she and her husband were forced to stay at a hotel. To her enjoyment and surprise they ended up having amazing sex, sometimes twice, every single night. Exhaling an exhilarated sigh of relief, she finally felt their sex life was back on track. Then the hotel stay ended. Confused and almost in tears, she admitted that as soon as they were back in the house, they went right back to their negative cycle: Sex stopped and the bickering resumed.

For those two weeks in the hotel, Rebecca and her husband were temporarily lifted out of their firmly entrenched domestic routine. All their pent-up frustrations vanished and they created a new sexual dynamic. Obviously, they desperately wanted to feel the same intimacy they'd had. When they were thrown back into their daily grind, their brains immediately switched back into the same old no-sex routine.

The Point: Change Is Never Fun But Is Worth It

Moving into married-woman sex means creating a new and unfamiliar sexual dynamic in your safe and comfortable world. Depending on your situation, a new and exciting sex life might mean revamping not only your sexual habits but also your daily minutiae. You have to negotiate these changes with your partner.

Next we need to look at the routine-turned-into-a-rut you've created in your bedroom.

WHAT IS YOUR SEX ROUTINE?

I want you to think about your very favourite supper—cost is no object. Would it be steak and lobster with a beautiful French wine? Use your imagination. The sky's the limit. Just to raise the stakes, let's say someone will do all the work for you so you don't have to worry about preparation or cleanup. Absolute heaven you think? Well yes, for the first little while.

Now I want you to think about eating this supper every night, seven days a week, 365 days a year for however long you've been with your partner. Do you think you might get tired of that wonderful meal? Why then is having the same single-woman sex over and over again any different? Just like having the same supper, having the same sex quickly comes to feel like, "Oh that *again*?!"

Over the first few years together, you and your partner gleefully fine-tuned sexual techniques that really worked for the two of you. However, just like too much of any good thing, having this wonderfully choreographed sex over and over again has taken away the sparkle, the zest, the zap. Once established, most people don't have any idea how to change the sex routine. And heck, with all the other responsibilities you have, when it comes to having sex, who wants to think that hard to come up with new and exciting ideas?

How rigid is your sexual routine? Can you easily bring new ideas, toys, or games into the bedroom, or is it simply too much work to initiate something new? Most couples go from a large sexual repertoire when they first get together to the act of sex becoming one or two standard positions and sex moves after only a few years together. This narrow sex focus is compounded by you being a creature of routine. Like most people, you gravitate to the safe and known. However, a set routine can deaden sexual fun because there is no room for spontaneity or adventure. Single-woman sex becomes boring because it's so darn predictable and mechanical: You rub me here, I'll rub you there, we'll have a little intercourse and we're done.

Your Sex Checklist

Do you sometimes feel like you have a sex checklist sitting by your bed?

- Sex is initiated.
- You don't feel like it but the guilt hanging over your head is too much to take.
- Unwillingly you drag yourself to bed.
- Undress—but not seductively because your partner might get the idea you want an extended sex session and you don't have the energy for that tonight.
- Kiss—oops sorry, kissing dropped off the list awhile ago. Too much effort and, if you can be quite honest, your partner forgets to brush his teeth before coming to bed and it's a huge turnoff.
- He fondles your breasts.
- You give his penis a little rub to get him going.
- Then he probably goes after your clitoris a little too aggressively—you want to tell him to back off but don't have the

energy to explain why he needs to stop treating your clit like it's some kind of remote control.

- If you're in a particularly good mood, you'll give him a little oral sex—with the caveat that you don't want to make him orgasm because you don't feel like swallowing tonight.
- After genitals have been sufficiently touched, you move on to intercourse. Assume first position.
- Three to four minutes of thrusting (and unless you can have a vaginal orgasm, this is the "wait it out" portion of sex).
- Assume second position.
- Three to four more minutes of thrusting (you're getting a little antsy so you start "helping" him to reach orgasm by showing some enthusiasm).
- For the grand finale, he gives a few hard thrusts, grunts, and gives his "I'm cumming now" moan.
- After a brief cuddle, he rolls over and sleeps.
- You're wide awake, still aroused.
- You feel resentful.
- Repeat every couple of weeks.

Even if this isn't your exact sex routine, chances are you have a similar checklist of what happens during your sexual experiences.

Sex Routine Trap

With the shift in life's priorities, there's already too much to think about to preplan sex. You're too mentally and emotionally paralyzed to initiate new ideas in the bedroom. The longer you've been with your partner, the more stuck you become in your routine.

THE DREADED MEMES

I admit that memes are a hot-button issue for me. It breaks my heart that the quality and quantity of your sexual experience has been scripted for you since birth; and unless you're a maverick, you have very little say on your sexual enjoyment. As a result, the sexual memes you unconsciously incorporated as "facts" can make or break whether you turn your present sexual situation around. Ironically, for having such a huge impact on your sex life, they are probably something you never heard about or even considered.

You might be asking, what exactly is a meme? The word *meme* comes from the word *memory* and according to Merriam-Webster's dictionary it's, "An idea, behavior, style, or usage that spreads from person to person within a culture." Said another way, memes are strongly held values or triggers within a culture that get passed down from generation to generation. Innocent memes include commercial jingles that you haven't heard for years but will immediately trigger your memory: "Where's the beef?," "I've fallen and I can't get up," "Plop, plop, fizz, fizz. Oh what a relief it is"; or turning on your car radio to hear a favourite old song that immediately takes you back ten years.

The scientific community considers memes a controversial and unproven theory. However, it's undisputable that you have deeply held beliefs around sexuality. For example, where do you stand on acquaintance rape, kissing on the first date, swinging, or age of consensual sex? Most likely you can answer immediately. But who or what helped you form these beliefs? You might assume that it was your parents and friends—and that would be absolutely true. Nevertheless, your beliefs around sexuality are a result of a much bigger, more pervasive societal ideology.

Memes are counterproductive when you start defining what is "appropriate" sexual conduct for you and everyone else around you. I bet if I asked why you don't boldly walk into a sex store and buy anything you want, you'd probably blush and mumble, "I don't know. I don't feel comfortable in that environment."

Intellectually, many modern women think that's a silly response. We are sexually emancipated, and walking into a sex store to buy whatever we want should not be a concern. Emotionally though, when we go to open the sex store's doors, our memes stop us in our tracks.

It may seem a tiny bit paranoid to accept that multiple people, things, or ideas are in bed with you and your partner. But it's true. Everything from big business, government, and religion create the type of sexual experience you have.

For example, pharmaceutical companies are changing the way we think and have sex with their multimillion-dollar erectile dysfunction pill campaigns. When President Ronald Reagan was running for re-election in 1984, he cut a deal with an influential religious organization. It agreed to give him its support in exchange for Reagan implementing, among other things, abstinence-only education in schools. Regardless of whether you agree or disagree with this, twenty years later we are witness to the devastating impact abstinence-only education has had on young people and their sexuality. One man's climb to success meant a deal with an influential voting group—as a consequence, millions of people's sexual health and happiness were compromised.

Another surprising influence in and outside the bedroom is how society still judges a girl's morality on whether she is a "Madonna" or a "whore." It's not uncommon to hear some fathers today (just like their fathers before) mockingly say, "Heaven help the poor guy who wants to date my daughter. He'll have to deal with me first." Meaning that if his daughter goes out and has sex, she will be marked as a whore; the dad wants his daughter to stay a Madonna. Along the same lines I've heard many people say of a pretty, young girl, "You better keep her locked up when she becomes a teenager or you'll be in trouble."

As you take this journey of changing your sexual situation, you must come to terms with the memes you have around your sexuality. You must determine whether they are getting in the way of you moving forward, or whether they really have had no impact on you whatsoever.

My guess is, like a massive boulder in the middle of the road, your memes will get in your way by inhibiting, scaring, and intimidating you not to move forward. Memes are tricky because they are unconsciously ingrained and comprise small beliefs that combine to have a distressing impact. A complex system of memes shows up in many forms:

- Why is it so hard to communicate your sexual needs?
- Why isn't it okay to want to have sex only a couple of times a month?
- Why does it bother you if he wants to look at porn?
- Why does the word *masturbation* immediately make your gut clench?
- Why do you consider letting loose being slutty?

Since birth you've been inundated with these messages. Don't expect to turn these beliefs anytime soon. But it's important for you to start paying attention.

Where Do You Start?

It's time to bring these unconscious belief systems to the surface. Start looking at how your sexuality is being affected by what society prescribes as proper. When you go out for coffee with your girlfriends, listen to what they say about sex. When you're reading your morning paper, critically assess what journalists report as sexual truths. When searching the Internet, be aware that most people who post things around sexuality are giving uneducated opinions (a big sore point for me). When you're listening to your mother/sister/aunt/friend espouse her wisdom, listen carefully. How do her views on sex differ from yours?

Soon, once you start looking, you'll see memes everywhere around you. Analyze what, if any, belief system curtails your sexuality.

CAN YOU SAY *VAGINA* OUT LOUD WITHOUT GIGGLING?

It's truly amazing that a couple can be together for fifty-plus years and have sex throughout that entire time and never once discuss their sex life—unless, of course, it's in negative terms. It makes a lot of sense then why so many couples end up having an unhappy sex life. No positive communication equals no opportunity to positively move sex forward, which can leave sex stagnant.

In a former life, I was a corporate trainer and taught employees how to communicate. In my opinion, teaching people nuclear physics would have been infinitely easier. Why? There are a million innuendoes to every individual's communication style, and thousands of reasons each interaction with another human being either works or breaks down. Not surprisingly, the one-size-fits-all crash course in effective communicating usually did very little to improve how those employees communicated and worked through their day-to-day politics. For the very same reason, that experience showed me that a "how to effectively communicate with your spouse" checklist won't work either.

I also learned that most people sincerely believe they are pretty good communicators and good-enough listeners. In fact, the majority of us, when faced with a difficult interaction, are pretty dismal communicators and even worse listeners.

Perhaps in your lifetime (maybe you are there right now), you will reach a place where you can easily say at the (childless) dinner table, "Let's mutually masturbate each other tonight" or, "I would like to try a new position that will hit my G-spot better" or, "Let's role-play superheroes." For the rest of us, getting to this place of absolute uninhibited sex talk is a long and winding road stretching out for our entire lives.

It's much easier to communicate when things are going well than when they are not. At this point in your relationship, your negative emotional loop works against your ability to have a good heart-to-heart talk. So read on a little more before broaching your difficult sex topics.

Instant Gratification Doesn't Work

We are a generation who expects instant gratification. We seek out the "ten easy steps to the best communication with your partner," a two-minute read that will immediately show impressive results of how to fix flagging sexual communication. However, we all know that doesn't work.

The Good News and the Not-So-Great News

So here's the good news and the not-so-great news about communication. We'll start with the not-so-great news: Good communication is a day-to-day, trial-and-error, constant vigilance that you'll probably never master in your lifetime. Learning to communicate well can be done only the old-fashioned way: by rolling up your sleeves and putting a lot of work into it.

Your beliefs and your partner's belief systems, or memes, around how you currently communicate are so deeply held that change may be slow. Most people who want the ten easy steps to great sexual communication get discouraged by a lack of instant progress so quit and revert to their old comfortable ways, digging themselves into a deeper single-woman-sex rut.

The good news: Learning how to communicate effectively, even in the stickiest situation, isn't difficult. The trick is being able to follow a set of guidelines and being willing to change. Without question, your effort will open up lines of communication and positively affect every aspect of your life.

Once Bitten, Twice Shy

Have you ever once had a "Honey, let's make our great sex life even better" conversation? Probably not. Instead, you tend to say something only when you're so unhappy it comes spewing out. You both get your defences up and the conversation goes quickly sideways. No wonder you avoid having these difficult conversations.

So don't beat yourself up for your lack of progressive sex communication. When faced with a difficult situation, most people try to avoid it. So, most likely, you've not had a lot of experience confronting your sexual issues head-on. Still, it's necessary for you to open up and be honest. The more comfortable you become, and the more practice you have dealing with difficult situations, the better you become at negotiating your way through them.

Facing Your Difficulties

When one person in a couple isn't happy with their sex life, they come to me—usually without their partner, so it's almost done in secret—complaining about their concern. My first response to their complaint is always, "Well, have you spoken to your partner about it?" More often than not, they become flustered and respond, "Once, a couple years back. Since then I don't know how to approach the topic without him (or her) getting all emotional on me." And although I appreciate the complexities of a relationship I think, "The only way you can do anything about this is to talk about it together instead of complaining to everyone but your partner."

I also see this when teaching couples' sexuality workshops. I start off the seminar by putting the men on one side of the room and the women on the other (kind of like a grade 7 dance). I give everyone a list of the top twenty-five bedroom issues couples face and ask each group to come up with the top three things that tick them off. Inevitably there's a great discussion within the segregated groups and, once lists are divulged, great discussions between the male and female groups. When couples are reunited and I ask them to discuss something on their list, the interaction momentum dives back to almost zero communication. It never ceases to amaze me how so many couples can discuss their sexuality woes with complete strangers and not with each other.

Getting Real with Your Sexual Communication

To get your sex life back on track, you need to know how your unproductive communication gets in the way. Your first assignment is to pay attention to your communication habits—good, bad, or indifferent. Think about the following:

1. What is your sexual complaint and what attempts have you made to have a productive conversation to help resolve this issue?
2. How often do you and your partner have conversations about your sex life?

3. Does talking about sex set you up for a big emotional explosion in a subject unrelated to sex (e.g., having a disagreement over not putting the toothpaste cap on properly)?
4. What sexual issues push your and your spouse's buttons?
5. What happens to your ability to listen when communication breaks down and disagreements begin?

Once you start recognizing your communication habits, it will be easier for you to productively work through them in Chapter 4.

YOUR FAVOURITE "NO SEX TONIGHT, DEAR" EXCUSE

Do you remember when you were a young girl? Our parents, in an effort to teach us responsibility, assigned us chores. Magically, an unexpected ailment afflicted us just as it was time to do them, "Mom, I'd really like to help clean out the basement but my leg is really sore and I don't think I should lift anything."

It's at this early point in our lives that many of us created poor habits to avoid "just doing it." We came up with every excuse under the sun to get out of what we felt forced to do. We spent twice as much time whining and procrastinating than it would have taken to simply do it.

Making excuses became a habit we continued into adulthood. For example, you know going to the gym for the forty-five-minute exercise class may be the best thing for you, but you're completely exhausted after an excruciatingly long day. You promise yourself, with your fingers crossed behind your back, you'll make up for it next time. Because we get so used to making excuses, they become second nature. We're able to justify our actions and convince ourselves that we're speaking the truth. Unfortunately, excuses don't stop at the bedroom door.

Women Convince Each Other That Excuses Are Okay
I was on the party bus returning home after speaking at a women's

weekend getaway. Everyone was partied out, sitting silently, so the entire bus heard one woman complain, "Shoot. When I get home my husband's going to want sex." Well, you should have heard the simultaneous, non-sexual groans that went up and down the aisle. Instantly the bus was buzzing, and the conversation for the next two hours between many of the girlfriends was about how they didn't have the will or energy to have sex after such a decadent weekend.

Eavesdropping on conversations, I heard every excuse under the sun why they shouldn't have to have sex. (Okay, I know, it wasn't my business to be eavesdropping, but I bet you couldn't have resisted either.) Fed up with hearing the conversations go round in circles, I asked three women why they simply didn't tell their partners they weren't up for sex that evening. They looked at me like I had three heads; I could tell they were thinking (but would never say to my face), "Sure, you're the big-shot Sex Expert who can easily talk about these sorts of things. It's far different with my husband. He'll freak out and start a fight. I don't want to end my happy weekend on that note." So instead the three women spent the rest of the trip inventing wild excuses why they couldn't have sex.

Excuses Lead to Procrastination Sex

According to Barry and Emily McCarthy's book *Rekindling Desire*, "Desire problems are the most frequent complaint of couples seeking sex therapy." Meaning, the feeling tired, being overtouched by children, I don't feel sexy thoughts that go on in your head play a big part in why you dread sex.

A big part of moving successfully into married-woman sex is knowing you're in control of the sexual experience and looking forward to it occurring. So, you need to start looking at the conscious or unconscious excuses you may be using to avoid sex.

Procrastination sex is making excuses and putting off sex until you absolutely have to have it. The art of procrastination sex goes something like this: You create a lot of good intentions to have sex, but when it comes time to execute, you talk yourself out of it with your preferred excuses. The more times you put sex off, the bigger the "failure" you become. Soon you start associating sex with being a failure. Not wanting to feel like a failure, the day you know you're going to have sex becomes a day filled with excuses as to why you can't do it: "I've got too much work to do," "I've got the kids' soccer practice," or "I've had such a busy week, I simply cannot peel my buttocks off the couch."

After that, it becomes easy to talk yourself out of having sex. You don't feel great about putting it off, yet you've built a wall of justifications. Ironically, when you do have sex, you might end up thinking, "Well, that wasn't so bad. I should do this more often."

When you allow yourself to get caught up in procrastination sex, your health, vitality, energy, and connection to your partner is slowly eroded—until you wake up one day feeling rotten and wondering how you and your partner drifted apart.

What Are Your Top Five Excuses?

You've got to come clean if you procrastinate to avoid sex. What excuses do you use to justify getting out of having sex? This section is a bit of tough love on my part. Although every one of these excuses is a legitimate concern, none is doing your sex life any favours:

- I have body issues that prevent me from relaxing while having sex.
- I have small children who take all my energy and time.
- I have small children and am all touched out.
- I am overwhelmed at work and am too stressed right now.
- I don't find my partner remotely sexy anymore.
- I resent doing the majority of the housework
- Sex is all about him—his wants, needs, and desires—and nothing to do with mine.
- I am exhausted.

Here are other ways you could be making excuses:

The Teaser: You make yourself available to have sex with your partner only when you know he won't be able to and can't do anything about it. You call him at work to say you're hot and bothered, knowing full well he can't leave the office. Or you make a play for sex when he is obviously too tired to see straight. Or you say you'd love to have sex even though you know he has a very important meeting the next day and needs to be rested and sharp. When your partner gets angry at you for not being interested in sex, you can throw it right back in his face how you tried to initiate and he wasn't interested.

Sex as a Reward: You tell your partner you're willing to have sex as long as your demands are met (e.g., you are rested, the kids are asleep, you aren't experiencing any PMS, etc.). These hurdles deaden the sexual experience, and your partner can never meet the needs on your list because at least one of these things is always occurring.

Let's Pretend It's Your Idea Not to Have Sex: If you don't like direct conflict, you may project what you are feeling and so it seems as if your partner is thinking or feeling it. For instance, you say as you drive by your favourite restaurant, "You seem hungry, we should grab something to eat" when it's you who's hungry. Or, "You've got to get up early tomorrow so you'd better get some sleep," because you aren't interested in having sex and want to appear as if it is your partner's idea to go to sleep.

Whatever your excuse, you need to pay attention to them. Once you understand how you talk yourself out of having sex, it is easier to stop the procrastination cycle.

KEY POINTS

1. The first step to understanding your sexual situation is to determine at what stage your relationship stands.
2. The energy and time that you put into your relationship will become the quality of your sex.

3. Your domestic bliss goes against being able to have a hot, erotic relationship.

4. Having sex becomes so routine you can check things off your sexual-encounter check-list.

5. Identify the memes that are getting in the way of good sex.

6. A great sex life means an open line of communication with your partner.

7. Excuses and talking yourself out of sex come in many forms: "I'm tired," "The kids might hear us," or "I've got a headache." It's all a ruse. Get real with how you inadvertently create procrastination sex.

CHAPTER 3

Getting Rid of Your Single-Woman-Sex Baggage

"Throughout your marriage you will fall in and out of love. In the bad times allow yourself to fall back in love. Don't hold on to grudges."

—Rudy de Bruin, married forty-one years with seven children

CREATING A NEW EMOTIONAL BOND

In the last chapter, we laid the foundation for you to stop avoiding and start addressing your sexual situation. Chapter 3 is about you venturing into the murky realm of your emotions. In this chapter you'll begin to detox your brain by leeching out your negative emotions toward sex.

Emotional Reactions

When someone does or says something to you, or something happens, you have an emotional (and sometimes physical) reaction. For example, someone does something nice, your emotional reaction is positive. When a person or situation cheeses you off, your emotional reaction is negative. While you're cruising through your day, your emotional reaction is neutral.

The Effects of Emotional Reactions

Emotional reactions follow similar principles to one law of physics: For every action, there will be an equal and opposite reaction.

Just as your daily routine is set in stone, so too are the majority of your emotional reactions. Your partner brings home flowers and after the initial feeling of "What did you do wrong?" you're delighted by his thoughtfulness. Your partner comes home and takes his bad day out on you, and you also get upset. He does something that really annoys you and you do nothing in return, biting your tongue and shoving down your angry feelings (you've learned that commenting on it just makes your life a lot more miserable).

So you wake up, see how your partner is feeling, make adjustments, and weave your way through the day accordingly. After a few years you both act and react to each other at an unconscious level. Often, even though you don't like how a situation plays out—especially when you disagree—you feel powerless to break out of the well-worn emotional reaction pattern.

Because you're still together, I assume that you have more positive or neutral bonding patterns than you do negative. The problem is when we take the happy and neutral interactions in stride—almost always forgetting them immediately—but the negative bonding patterns linger. This is especially true for women; we tend to hang on and remember the bad moments more so than men. Sexual difficulties, in particular, bring up a lot of negative emotions and linger longer in our memory than neutral or happy sexual interactions.

Because single-woman sex is so limited, it throws you into a sexual routine that results in negative emotional reactions. It's the cringe factor to sex: Sex is initiated and your reaction is to cringe. You need to determine your negative emotional reaction toward sex so you can understand how much brain detoxification will be needed.

To do this, we'll look at your reaction to sex once it's initiated.

THE BELL CURVE OF SEXUALITY

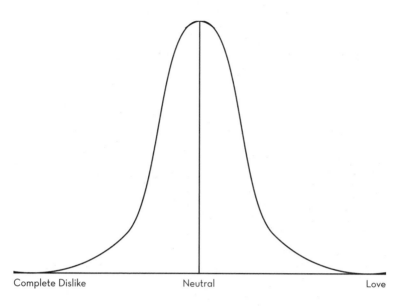

Complete Dislike   Neutral   Love

Right Side

On the right side of the bell curve of sexuality would be women who absolutely love, love, love sex. Fatima (she's a real person—this is not an exaggerated or made-up story), has been married for seventeen years, has a thriving therapy practice, and two children. She volunteers and is in general a pretty active lady. Every single day of her marriage she has had sex, with or without her period, sometimes on her own—remember, sex doesn't always mean intercourse. After I picked my jaw up off the ground, she explained it's her way of relaxing, her treat, her feel-good method to get through the day.

Lorna is on this same end of the bell curve, and gets downright grouchy if she doesn't get sex on a regular basis. She's works full-time and is raising two kids. More than once, after she unnecessarily snapped at me, I requested, "Would you please just go and get some sex for everyone's sanity?"

Left Side

On the extreme left side of the bell curve are those women who have a tremendous aversion toward sexuality. They really don't want to have sex again for the rest of their lives. Some have experienced a sexual trauma such as rape or incest. Others had an upbringing that programmed them to believe enjoying sex was the ultimate no-no. Some women have muscular and skeletal issues that can be a source of pain during sex. Some women's vaginas tense up so much that they don't allow for intercourse (the technical term is vaginismus).

You may believe that you completely dislike sex yet compared to what women who experience physical or emotional trauma are going through, your dislike of sex is a completely different kettle of fish; most likely you do like sex, but have a ton of built-up negative emotions. So, yes, you would likely place yourself closer to the left-hand side, but that doesn't mean you never want to have sex for the rest of your life.

Middle

The majority of us sit somewhere in the middle of the curve. You like sex when you're in the mood, don't feel pressured, and don't feel guilty or resentful. The tricky part is saying exactly where on this bell curve you sit. The more negative baggage you carry around the act of sex, the more left of centre you place yourself.

Still not sure? What is your initial gut reaction when your partner initiates sex? Is it, "Super, let's run to bed and jump into the sack—I can hardly wait to have sex with you"? That would put you to the right of centre. Or is it, "I'm tired but it sounds like something I could get into"? That would put you in the middle. Or is it, "Oh no, has it been a week already? I really don't want to. I don't feel like it, but I don't want to listen to him complain so I'll just get it over with"? That would put you to the left of centre.

So wherever you are on the bell curve, your objective is to move your emotional reaction pattern toward sex to the right. To do this, you must work through your emotional baggage.

Don't Go inside Your Head

Before venturing into the rest of this chapter, a word of caution: Don't "go inside your head." Be careful not to put on your intellectual thinking cap and profess, "Yes, yes, yes, I know this stuff already." Of course you know this stuff. However, you must keep asking yourself, "What am I actually putting into action in my day-to-day life?"

So please don't simply peruse this chapter. Putting some time and effort into this section will see you and your partner creating a strong foundation for a great sex life.

FEAR ISN'T SEXY

What fears do you unintentionally allow to hamper a great sex life? Insecurity, jealousy, and rejection are just a few that get in the way of a couple fully enjoying sex.

These and other fears slowly chip away at your sexual self-esteem. Because the wearing away of your sexual self-confidence is so gradual, these fears usually aren't noticed until it's too late. You need to ask yourself how you've unwillingly allowed fear to take over your bedroom happiness.

Fear Is Not Your Sexual Friend

Fear manifests itself in emotions you would never associate with it: anger, guilt, pride, anxiety, depression, inhibition, and shame.

Therefore, when something in your relationship pushes your fear buttons, you may not feel the wild thumping of your heart, shortness of breath, or fight-or-flight feelings associated with pure fear. Instead, you will get angry, feel guilty, become extremely anxious, or maybe get depressed.

Although you've felt all of these negative emotions at one time or another, you have your own way of expressing fear, such as anxiety. Why is that significant? Knowing your own way of expressing fear makes it easier for you to identify and start dealing with it.

When you feel fear, in any of its guises, you likely do your utmost to get control of the situation.

Control—Friend or Foe?

Having and being in control seems to be critical for many busy women. And really, what choice do you have? Our fast-paced society places high expectations on how we "should" live our lives, and there's no speed bump in sight. Your life would be completely chaotic if you didn't structure it.

Control is necessary—in moderation. Exerting too much control, however, gives you a false sense that you've got a handle on things. Plus, you don't allow people or things to settle and sort themselves out on their own.

Chances are your negative feelings toward sex trigger your fear. Because you feel fear, your insecurities around your sex life force you to exert control. So when both you and your partner feel insecure (worried that everything is going to fall apart) instead of having an open and honest heart-to-heart about the state of your sexuality (because the past has shown you only disagree when you bring up the topic) you muffle your insecure feelings by taking control.

Here's an example of what this can look like for women.

Problem: She feels resentment from an inequitable distribution of household chores.

Insecurity: She doesn't feel confident enough to bring up her need for her partner to do his fair share or how to be more assertive when she tries to discuss this with him.

Fear: She's afraid that speaking her piece about the household chores will start another fight. She feels anger that there's too much work and not enough day.

Control: Because she doesn't feel like she has control over the inequitable distribution of household chores, she exerts control over the one thing she can: sex.

Here's an example of what this can look like for men.

Problem: He wants more sex.

Insecurity: He, like most men, sees a rift in sex as a rift in the overall relationship, and he feels insecure that it's not working or is fading away.

Fear: He gets afraid and angry that she never seems to want sex. He feels depressed, "Is this what the rest of my life is going to look like?"

Control: Starts to nag and put pressure to have sex more often.

Control means a lack of flexibility to see things from another point of view. The more control you need to exhibit to the outside world, the less control you feel inside yourself. Ask yourself why you need to be holding the reins so tight. What is it that makes you feel so insecure that you can't ease up?

Control Freaks, Stand Up and Be Counted

Hello, my name is Trina and I'm a control freak. I'm not proud of the fact and yet it's a part of my personality. Which is fine, but unfortunately my husband also has the control-freak gene. And boy, have we had our share of power struggles over the years. A lot of "I'm right" disagreements outside our bedroom stopped me wanting to have sex with him inside our bedroom (or anywhere else, for that matter).

You may not be a control freak like me, but I believe all of us, to some extent or another, need to have control of at least one area of our life. Where you exert too much control is likely what you feel most insecure about.

Power struggles stem from a lack of control, which stems from fear. What got you stuck in the single-woman-sex rut has a lot to do with your fears.

"Oh No You Didn't" Power Struggles

Naturally, trying to control another person and their actions will turn him or her into a victim. This controller-victim pattern manifests itself in power struggles. Power struggles inside the bedroom then reflect those that you experience outside the bedroom. For instance, couples who have different sex drives constitutes a major power struggle: the person who wants less sex is the person in control, while the person who wants more sex becomes the victim.

Most people who want less sex think it's the other way around. They feel the other person is controlling them and trying to make them feel guilt. You see, the person who wants less sex is controlling how much, when and why sex occurs. The person who wants sex more feels his or her ability to have sex has been taken hostage.

Relationships plagued by control and authority issues are characterized by day-to-day battles such as how much money is spent, what activities children are allowed to do, or which set of in-laws to visit during the holidays. Rarely is any issue spared.

Not surprisingly, many of these power struggles land smack dab in the middle of having sex. Usually a power struggle over sex is cover for not dealing with a bigger power struggle outside the bedroom. If you have a power struggle over how often you have sex, chances are you're also having control issues about everything from what the kids eat for breakfast to how often his mother comes to visit. You have to work on your bigger issues of control before you can work on isolated difficulties, and therefore you will need to address the larger issues before you can resolve the sexual issues. Trying to separate sexual issues in the midst of major control and inequality issues will fail because it simply transfers the combat zone.

Power struggles = "rights" fights
Power struggles = a lack of resolution or negotiation
Power struggles = poor sex and no intimacy

Every relationship is a balancing act. In perfect balance, both partners have the security of the other's love and are equal in several ways: their emotional investment in the relationship, their attractiveness to each other, and the number of needs each fills for the other. Neither feels suffocated or emotionally shortchanged, and neither is inclined to take the other for granted. You're okay with yourself, your partner, and your relationship exactly the way it is. Nice in theory, but I'm not sure how realistic complete relationship balance is. It's definitely something to strive for but never something to expect.

Become aware of what makes you feel angry, guilty, anxious, inhibited, or ashamed. See how these bring out your insecurities, which may lead you to exert control over your partner, your relationship and ultimately your sex life. Productively working through these feelings and the control issues that lead to power struggles will be covered in Chapter 5.

For now, let's dig a little deeper by seeing how shame, blaming, and flaming keep you in this fear cycle.

SHAME, BLAME, FLAME

A Lovely "He's Wrong" Fairy Tale

Once upon a time, your partner confessed that it was his fault your sex life was in the toilet. You compassionately forgave and enlightened him with some clever and well-thought-out ideas. With great affection, you supervised his progress, lovingly encouraged him, forgave the occasional fall off the recovery wagon, gently pushed him back on, and tenderly showed him that every step of the way—though he was misguided and you were ultimately right—everyone is human and makes mistakes.

You thrived and shone in your new role, and he, seeing his improvements and seeing how happy you were, also thrived. After he made all the needed changes, your sex life magically turned into something you both want. Happy in sex once again, like when you first got together, the two of you rode off into the sunset and lived sexually ever after. The end.

Although this is a fairy tale, it's time to admit there's a considerable amount of finger pointing as to why your sex life isn't a finely tuned machine. And, yes, your partner is doing as much finger pointing back, but does the justification make it any better? Repeat after me, "I cannot change my partner; I can change only myself. And being a victim by shaming, blaming, and flaming is not going to help me get out of this mess I've helped create."

It's time to come clean and figure out what are you doing to keep the destructive shame/blame/flame momentum going in your relationship? How have you avoided taking responsibility and blaming your partner for what's going on in your sex life? What have you been doing to sabotage sexual success?

What Is the Shame/Blame/Flame Cycle?

When we feel shame around our sex lives, it's likely we're dealing with feelings of insecurity or low self-esteem. As we discussed in the previous section, instead of taking responsibility for our stuff, we take those negative emotions and throw them onto our partner. We blame him for how we are feeling. Since in our eyes he is at fault for how we feel, we create fights or "flame" him.

Let's say you would like more foreplay. Trouble is, you don't have the confidence to express what you want in words. Instead, it's easier to convey your needs, wants, and desires by believing that your partner (1) can read your mind as to what makes you happy, (2) understands that your passive-aggressive sighing means you don't have an on/off switch, and (3) gets that your moving his hands is teaching him a new technique. You are genuinely shocked when he doesn't get your hinting.

Hurt, angry, and humiliated, you feel shame that you went out on a limb to convey what you wanted sexually. But instead of taking responsibility for not giving him a good enough explanation, you blame him for not being sensitive enough to your needs. To keep the peace, you bottle up your feelings until one day you feel particularly low. You find that he hasn't put the toothpaste cap on properly/didn't put the garbage out/said something you didn't appreciate. Whatever his folly, you've had enough of his crap and it's time to flame him.

Blindsided, your partner throws it right back at you. You feel more shame, so you throw more blame onto your partner and, naturally, stoke the flames even further. Nobody wins. Everyone loses. The satisfaction and quality of sex takes a nose-dive. Day-to-day living somehow becomes about self-preservation—not allowing the other person to hurt you. Where you once were a team, now you are two individuals duking it out, a mini-war of me against you.

Let's break down the shame/blame/flame cycle to better understand how it affects your sex.

Shame

Shame starts with guilt. Guilt means feeling remorse that you are responsible for some offence—whether you committed that offence or just that you feel responsible for it. Guilt is closely linked with inferiority and shame. Both inferiority and shame help you feel guilty over and over and over again—long after the "offence" has passed.

One study showed more than 90 per cent of women and men who had negative sexual experiences in their past blamed themselves for something they didn't cause.

Sources of shame can include:

Masturbation
Sexual fantasies
Being sexually rejected or ridiculed
Having made a poor choice in partner
Having a sexual dysfunction
Having a sexually transmitted infection
Receiving obscene phone calls
Being sexually harassed
Major traumas such as sexual abuse, incest, rape
Staying in a loveless marriage
Not being able to stop the terrible arguments

It's hard to shake shame, so it follows us around and rears its ugly head when we are feeling insecure.

Blame

While engaged, I read a string of books on how to have a successful marriage. Looking back, it was, for the most part, a futile exercise as my husband and I were still in the newbie, lovey-dovey stage. However, in among all my "that will never happen to us because we've got our relationship together" righteousness, one tidbit carried me through when we were on the verge of separation: Successful couples resolve their issues instead of blaming each other for their unhappiness.

In John Gottman and Nan Silver's fabulous book *The Seven Principles to Making Marriage Work*, they found that a key characteristic to a successful relationship is how couples do their best to resolve their issues before they escalate. Gottman and Silver came to this conclusion by filming more than 700 couples living in a makeshift staged home. After observing couples interact for a few hours, the authors were able to predict with 95 per cent accuracy whether or not the couple would be able to stand the test of time. The authors found that couples who resolved their issues were most likely to have a happy marriage. This is true regardless of the issue's immensity or the couple's frustration or anger.

If you are blaming your partner, look at what's not working in your relationship, it's likely a cluster of small unresolved issues that have built up over time. You lumped all these smaller problems together and determined that "I don't feel like having sex anymore." Because no longer feeling like you want to have sex is a big problem, it becomes overwhelming to resolve.

Flame

"I don't want to have sex" becomes the focal point for flaming each other. Because it is such a tender issue, you do your best not to fan those flames and avoid any discussion of it. But the unresolved blaming lingers, so you both take tiny digs that create more problems that go unresolved.

Many couples balk at resolving the mini-digs, feeling like a condescending schoolteacher by saying, "When you rolled your eyes at me during breakfast it really hurt my feelings." Or, "Babe, I got defensive when you crossed your arms and sighed." It seems to be too much effort. So we drop it. But as Gottman and Silver discovered in their research, these issues fester and grow.

What Can You Do?

When the two of you are in this shame/blame/flame negative cycle, you find your partner barely tolerable and at times extremely irritating. You have to come back to being a team. This can be done only by figuring out who's blaming whom for what. Stop the shame/blame/flame cycle by sticking to the facts when you argue. Let's take a look at how you can begin to easily resolve your issues.

JUST THE FACTS, MA'AM, JUST THE FACTS

Have you ever sat back and wondered why disagreements around sex get you so angry? It's because there is so much emotion tied in with fighting.

Facts, on the other had, are the cool oasis in the hot desert of your disagreements. Facts help you to have constructive conversations with your partner about your sexual needs. Facts allow you to navigate and not allow your sex life to stay stagnant.

You can work through your negative baggage without hurting feelings. The shame/blame/flame cycle is based on your emotional response, not logic or facts. Bringing the facts into your "marital discussions" means relearning how to assess your present sexual challenges. It's time to look at your disagreements with a new set of eyes.

Three Sides to Your Arguments

How you perceive the world is neither right nor wrong; it's simply your perception.

Your partner has a different set of life experiences and therefore sees the world through a different set of eyes. For example, has your partner ever got himself completely tied up like a pretzel, while you stood back unaffected, thinking, "Hey, Chicken Little, the sky's not falling"? You are both looking at the same situation from two very different perspectives. Accordingly, you both have very different emotional responses to the single event.

Just because you are experiencing the same sex life doesn't mean you are seeing it from the same perspective. And therein lies the problem: When you and your partner look at why things have gone wrong with your sex life you see it from two totally different perspectives. It shouldn't be a stretch then to say for every single sexual situation you encounter there will be a three-sided argument: your side, your partner's side, and the facts.

On top of this, the longer you avoid and deny and let unresolved disagreements fester, the more difficult it will be to understand each other's perceptions. Your ultimate goal is to see the problem from the same perspective; otherwise, you'll keep circling the same old problem without ever finding resolution.

Emotions versus Fact

To turn your sexual situation around, you have to take a long hard look at what's been created then separate the facts from your emotions. When looking at their sexual situation people tend to pull out the few facts that support their argument and add a liberal dose of their emotional interpretation.

Conversely, when you're examining facts there's no right or wrong; it's simply what's so. Most people find it hard to face up to facts because in most every disagreement each person is half the cause.

A disagreement using only the facts will conclude quickly and will never haunt your relationship again. Let's take a look at how this works.

Susan and Brian's Story

Susan and Brian were trapped in single-woman sex and their arguments cycled in and out of embarrassment, guilt, blame, and resentment. Susan was completely turned off by Brian's incessant pressure to have sex. Brian, who had a hard time initiating, was sick and tired of always being rejected. Because they didn't know what else to do, they went into a negative emotional pattern of attack-counterattack—one blaming and the other putting up a wall of emotional alienation. Divorce was often bandied about; the same old hurtful battles got dredged up over and over again while all affectionate touch was nonexistent.

Luckily Susan's best friend encouraged her to seek counselling. After a few weeks of stomping around, Brian finally consented to go with Susan. When the counsellor asked them separately what they were so angry about, it became clear their anger was a thin guise for all their hurt. Anger and blaming protected them from experiencing sadness and loneliness.

When you look at Susan and Brian's situation, they are experiencing the same sex but looking at it with two different perspectives. As such, both are entrenched in their justifications as to why they are the victim of their circumstance. Disagreements became a matter of going around in circles, trying to show the other why their perspective was more justified. They were fighting emotional fights and not factual fights.

Let's take a look at the facts:

1. Brian is shy and unassertive in initiating sex.
2. Brian initiated sex late at night when Susan was tired and uninterested.
3. Susan did not like the way Brian initiated even though she was not comfortable with initiating sex herself.
4. Susan wanted romance, and to be seduced by Brian.
5. Brian did not feel comfortable or confident in the seducer role because he was only ever taught how to have single-woman sex.
6. Susan had previous bad experiences in her premarital sexual encounters that affected her ability to relax during sex.

Once the counsellor was able to separate the facts from emotions, it became easier to offer solutions. With their counsellor's help Brian and Susan formed a step-by-step plan on how they wanted to move forward. Here are a few concrete, doable things they were able to implement immediately:

1. Both had to stop threatening divorce.
2. Both agreed to immediately stop when they caught each other fighting old battles.
3. Both agreed to stop looking at how their relationship was wrong and start focusing on what they wanted: increased emotional and sexual intimacy.
4. Both agreed to start affectionate non-sexual touch to get their good feelings back.

It's Your Turn to Play the Emotions versus Facts Game

The next time you have a disagreement (not that I'm encouraging you to fight, but it's probably inevitable) use this test to know whether you're using facts or emotions. If your argument uses facts, the discussion will be short and to the point. Even the most complex situation can be summarized factually in less than two minutes. When you are predominately using emotions, you cling to as few facts as you can to make your case. You can go on, and on, and on about why you're right. But as you go on and on, you can feel your emotions and blood pressure rising.

Do your best to make it a learning experience when you fall into a disagreement. Instead of thinking, "You're such a jerk" (add curses as you see fit), take a step back and think, "Hmm. Why is this pushing my buttons? Perhaps I need to understand the facts instead of letting my emotions get the best of me." Be as objective as possible. Be clear how both of you are fuelling your disagreement by throwing around emotions.

Places to Find the Facts

1. Figure out what your hot-button issues are. That is, look for and listen for the topics that cause you to fly off the handle or get bent out of shape, like, "You never want to have sex."
2. Notice your body's reaction. Do you tense up? Pull away? Start to disassociate? Hold your breath? These are all tied in with your emotional reaction to the hot-button topic.
3. Why does this topic push your buttons?
4. What buttons is it pushing—guilt, frustration, anger, anxiety?
5. Take a step back and figure out what is occurring in this situation (e.g., your partner complains you never have sex. The fact is that you two are having sex once a month, which is good for you and not satisfying for your partner.)

Remember, in a disagreement you always have two choices: go down the well-worn road of emotional reaction, which inevitably creates a huge fight. Or take the high road, own up to what you created, and figure out the facts—creating a quick, clean resolution.

WRAP-UP

This was a pretty heavy chapter. I appreciate that coming to terms with all of the negative emotional baggage you built up is not easy. Yet the best way to toss what you don't want is to face your fear. I applaud your courage.

It's time to let go of your negative baggage and show you how to enjoy sex once again. We'll start with creating better communication between the two of you.

KEY POINTS

1. How much negative baggage you carry around determines how much work you have to do. Where did you rate yourself on the sexual bell curve?

2. Unhappy sex is rarely about sex, it is about the power struggles outside the bedroom. What control/victim games are you playing with your partner?

3. How much of your sex life do you blame your partner for? If you are serious about getting great sex, you must stop blaming him and take responsibility for your part.

4. When you are disagreeing, stick to the facts and don't allow your emotions to run the show.

CHAPTER 4

Talking to Him about Sex

"Most couples don't talk *about* sex; they talk *around* sex. They communicate through gestures, veiled comments, euphemisms, winks, sighs, gibes, jokes, put-downs, lies, and code words. At times the way they communicate is more harmful to the relationship than not talking at all."

—Patricia Love, Ph.D., *Hot Monogamy*

YOUR COMMUNICATION: THE GOOD, THE BAD, AND THE UGLY

Now that you've waded through the unpleasant part, it's time to figure out how to tell your beloved things are going to have to change ... for the better. By working together the two of you will have some great times, not only in the foreseeable future, but also well into your twilight years. Sounds pretty wonderful, doesn't it? It is—until you go to have your first conversation.

Because your sexual situation, ability to communicate, and emotional baggage are unique, giving a one-size-fits-all approach to better communication won't work. The following pages provide many ways to communicate better. Read through this chapter and then pick one technique. Think about the technique; discuss with your partner how you want to implement it; then put the technique into practice. Once you master it, move on to the next one.

Let's Start at the Start

Communication is the cornerstone of any good relationship, especially when it comes to a couple's sexual satisfaction. I often feel like a broken record saying to people, "The best way to work through any sexual difficulty is through open, honest, heartfelt communication."

You've probably flipped through magazine articles explaining how couples can best communicate, glanced over the communication techniques, and mumbled to yourself that you already know this stuff. You've walked away from the information, never implementing a single technique. And then, you are extremely frustrated because you and your partner have such a hard time communicating.

But now the sexual stakes are higher. You're playing for your lifelong sexual happiness. Good communication means practising a technique over and over again until you are comfortable with it. Unless you make a concerted effort to turn your sexual communication around, very little is going to change in your sexual dynamics.

From this point forward, your communication is not about rehashing everything is wrong; rather, you need to focus and be assertive about on how you want your sex life to be. Assertive communication will help you create a trusting environment where excellent sex communication is easy—yes, even in the middle of a disagreement.

The Flow of Communication

Like most, you probably don't know how to start this conversation. Here are general guidelines for bringing up and then working through your sexual issues:

1. Understand how you presently communicate (i.e., passively or aggressively).

2. Raising the "Our Sex Needs to Change" Topic.

3. Work through outstanding issues that are getting in the way of you having a productive conversation around sex (i.e., inequitable distribution of household chores).

4. Tell your partner what good sex means to you (Chapter 6).

5. Have an ongoing, lifelong conversation about the state of your sex life. (Chapter 7, 8 and 9).

1. UNDERSTAND HOW YOU PRESENTLY COMMUNICATE

What Kind of Communicator Are You?

It goes without saying that most arguments happen because you are angry. You get angry because you feel out of control in the situation. Therefore, you try to regain control either through passive or aggressive communication. Passive people do not say what they want, and aggressive people tend not to take the other person's feelings into consideration. Both passive and aggressive people are considering only their feelings, not the health of the couple.

Passive Communicators

Communication pitfall: Your opinion counts, mine doesn't. Passive communicators have a tendency to keep their mouths shut and say things like, "It's fine," "Don't worry about it," or "Whatever." Silence and projecting guilt are the way these people punish others.

Your partner initiates sex. You are not in the mood but feel guilty. You don't know how to express your frustration so you keep your mouth shut. You lie back and are less than enthusiastic. Deep down you want him to notice, stop the sex, and say, "I can see by your lacklustre performance that you're not happy with having sex. Let's just cuddle instead." When that doesn't happen, you punish him by staying silent or mumbling a sarcastic "That was great."

Aggressive Communicators

Communication pitfall: My opinion counts, yours doesn't. **Aggressive** does not mean threatening. Aggressive communicators don't have any trouble telling the other person how they feel—and then some. There isn't much room, if any, for the partner's point of view.

Your partner initiates sex. You are not in the mood and start winding up to tell him exactly why. You explain to him that using guilt to get his way isn't going to work and that if he ever wants sex again he better just put it back in his pants for now.

Why Passive and Aggressive Styles Don't Help Successful Communication

With both passive and aggressive communication, conversations turn into an "I'm right/you're wrong," "someone's going to win/someone's going to lose" power play. Each of you will do everything to win this conversation, so nothing gets resolved. You and your partner go round in circles with the same fight, and it gets pushed down again. Unresolved arguments slowly simmer and then come to a boil. Eventually, you can't take it anymore and snap.

When passive communicators snap, they tend to be manipulative, dig in their heels, throw out sarcastic zingers, and refuse to cooperate. When aggressive communicators snap, they yell, scream, and generally blow a gasket. Both are equally destructive to a relationship.

Assertive Communicators

Communication style: Both your opinions, feelings, and circumstances count. Each and every assertive communication is based in fact and accounts for both your perspectives. It's all about *what can I do that is best for us, not just for myself?*

When you've taken the time to understand the other person's point of view and have clearly stated what is going on with you, negotiation will easily happen. Why? Because both of you have taken the time to understand the other's circumstance. Figuring out a solution becomes a team effort instead of a battle of wills.

2. RAISING THE "OUR SEX NEEDS TO CHANGE" TOPIC

It's understandable when it comes time for you to have the "our sex needs to change" conversation you stop dead in your tracks. Where do you start? How do you bring this up without it starting a humongous disagreement? What if you raise the issue and he is in no way interested in changing? Don't let these or other fears scare you out of initiating this extremely important conversation.

Face-to-face communication is always best, but sometimes writing down your thoughts can be an effective way to break the ice. It allows you to think about what you want to say, put your thoughts in logical order, and communicate the things that are initially usually too difficult to say out loud. Your best start may be to write an e-mail. Remember, you need to follow up your correspondence with a face-to-face talk.

Here's an Idea of What to Say or Write to Break the Ice.

"Sex isn't what it used to be and it's probably safe to say both of us would like that to change. We've been having trouble for "X" years. Neither of us is happy. When we've tried to talk about sex, it's ended up in a fight. I don't want to disagree anymore. I want us to have a mutually beneficial sex life. Problem is, up until this point, I haven't allowed myself to be an equal in the bedroom. Please don't take issue with this, because I'm not pointing the finger of blame at you.

"In order for me to once again be an enthusiastic bedtime partner, we need to work through a few unresolved issues. I have all the confidence that we can do this. After that we need to create a new and better way to have sex. Your needs and wants are important and so are mine. In order for me to have fun and enjoy sex on an ongoing basis, we need to change some of the ways we're having sex.

"We both need to make concessions in order to have a sex life that works for both of us.

"For now, we need to make a truce that when we discuss issues relating to our sex, we do our best to work our way to a resolution—instead of going in circles. Let's talk about this tonight.

"I love you and look forward to once again having a great sex life."

Once you start this new way of communication in motion, it's time to troubleshoot what can go wrong and how to fix it.

3. WORK THROUGH OUTSTANDING ISSUES THAT ARE GETTING IN THE WAY OF YOU HAVING A PRODUCTIVE CONVERSATION AROUND SEX

Why Your Communication Goes Sideways

When you look at how you and your partner disagree, it's little wonder your communication breaks down and isn't resolved. Here's the step-by-step model of how you likely have an unproductive conversation:

- You've reached your boiling point and decide to bring up the issue with your partner.
- You provide lots of pent-up emotion, with a smidgen of fact to help you feel justified in venting your feelings with hostility.
- You have no respect for your partner's situation or point of view.
- You value only the impact on you.
- You need to defend your view and be right because your partner just doesn't understand or get what you're trying to tell him.
- You provide more details about the impact on you.
- If all else fails, you provide more detail about the impact on you.
- There is no resolution—you or your partner walk away in a huff.

Here's this model in action. Hitomi is an aggressive communicator while Frank is a passive communicator. (Please note: If it's not housework you're disagreeing about, feel free to insert whatever issue you are grappling with, like money, work, in-laws, etc. I'm using housework as an example because it seems to be a pretty common issue among busy couples.)

Hitomi: Can we talk?

Frank: Sure. [with a shrug and sigh]

Hitomi: Why do you think the house and kids are my responsibility even though my job is as demanding as yours? Yes, you help, but only if I ask. I'm not your mother and I shouldn't have to nag. The division of labour is unfair. If one of the children is sick it's me who has to find child care or stay home from work. You would never think about taking time off.

Frank: [cold stare, arms crossed] Are you starting this again? I don't feel like talking about this. [under his breath] You're not exactly perfect either.

Hitomi: I don't believe it! Every time I bring something up you turn the discussion into what's wrong with me. How come it's always about me and never about you? It always becomes something that is bothering you. [Notice how, even though Hitomi is aggressive, she feels Frank is in control of the conversation.]

Does this conversation sound familiar? It's probably the reason you avoid the conversations you need to have—and then resent sex when it's initiated.

Let's look at how you can turn your communication around.

Here's How Your Communication Should Look

Proper communication is a constant balancing act of taking responsibility for your part, looking at your partner's perspective, clearly and factually stating your perspective, then being open to negotiating a conclusion.

- A small issue has arisen and you deal with it while it's still fresh.
- Go in knowing you are at least half responsible for your current sexual situation. Show respect for your partner's situation or point of view (notice how his point of view needs to be put before your own). Your partner has his own ideas regarding what good sex means. But when most people are angry they don't try

to understand where the other person is coming from. Remember, you need to create a resolution that also meets his needs.

- Clearly and factually state your current situation.
- Most of us are not clear, specific, and factual enough when we explain what we feel. When we are defensive or in an established relationship, we tend to use a communication shorthand to explain. That is, we skip and assume that our partner knows exactly what we're talking about. If your partner keeps disagreeing with you because he's missed the point, it's probably because he wasn't given a good enough explanation.
- State how the situation has an impact on you and your ability to be sexual.
- Do your best to resolve the issue immediately. A general rule is to resolve your conflicts within twenty-four hours. Yes, of course, you'll need a cool-down period. There's a reason for the old adage "Don't go to bed mad."
- Come to a mutually beneficial resolution.

Hitomi:	Can we talk?
Frank:	Sure. [with a sigh]
Hitomi:	I appreciate you have a great deal on the go these days. The thing is, so do I. And I need to ask, what would you do if you were me?
Frank:	What do you mean?
Hitomi:	I'm feeling overwhelmed with having all the responsibilities of the house, kids, and my full-time job. I need you to help me more.
Frank:	Like what?
Hitomi:	[comes to the conversation prepared with a list of things she would like him to do] I've thought this through and here are some chores I would like you to do to help me out.
Frank:	[reading over the list and getting a bit defensive] That's a lot of chores.

Hitomi: [getting a little defensive] Yes, and this is why I feel so overwhelmed when I go to bed every night. What would you consider a reasonable request?

Frank: [taken off guard] I don't know.

Hitomi: Do you need some time to think about it?

Frank: [silence with a ticked-off look]

Hitomi: Look, I need your input in order to resolve this.

Frank: [more silence]

Hitomi: Okay. I can see I've come at you with a lot to think about. I'll leave this list with you and we can discuss this tomorrow once you've had a chance to think about it.

Frank: Fine. [in a tone that means it is anything but fine]

Just because Hitomi and Frank are having an assertive communication doesn't mean they will not feel anger or frustration. The difference is they are working toward a resolution instead of having the conversation go around in circles.

Most men need direct and specific ideas to understand what you mean/need, instead of saying, "I need your help around the house," Hitomi came prepared with a list of factual, specific list to give Frank an idea of what she needed.

This is where women comment, "But with two people working, why is he 'helping her' rather than being in a partnership that should be equal (splitting chores and child care right down the middle). She's being put in the position of having to ask him, meaning he could refuse. She's having to justify why he needs to help her (not the marriage/family)." It's been my experience—although certainly not always the case—that people will react positively toward the phrase "Can you help me" rather than "You need to do/change this".

That being said, when you bring up the topic, regardless if you use "help," "please" or "thank you," there will be resistance to change. Therefore, there has to be some motivation for him to want to change. In the above situation, we're assuming that when Frank lightens the household duty load for Hitomi, she will feel more rested. Which for

Frank will mean she will come to bed not as tired, translating to her being more into the sexual act. If Frank does start helping more with the chores and Hitomi still doesn't want sex, Frank will (justifiably) feel ripped off.

So let's get back to this conversation and how Hitomi can bring the topic up again the next day.

Conversation the next day.

Both Hitomi and Frank have had a chance to think and cool down. Although there will be some lingering emotions, Hitomi raising the topic again is best done when both are in a neutral state of mind.

Hitomi: Do you have five minutes to talk about the list I gave you yesterday?

Frank: [looking like he wants to do anything but] I was just about to do something.

Hitomi: [getting perturbed because she feels he is avoiding the conversation] Okay, when's a better time?

Frank: [with a shrug and irritated sigh] Later.

Hitomi: Look, Frank, I understand you've got a busy day and yet we need to talk about this sometime in the next few days. We both know you would like sex more often. Did it ever occur to you that I want us to be closer too? That's why I'm doing my best to come up with a solution. In order for that to happen, we need to sit down and have this conversation.

Frank: What does me doing chores have to do with us having sex?

Hitomi: It's really difficult for me to get into sex when I'm exhausted and have a million to-do's going on in my head. You helping out will take some of the pressure away. That way I can come to bed more relaxed.

Frank: I don't have time to do what's on your list.

Hitomi: I appreciate that it seems overwhelming. Realistically it will be thirty to forty-five minutes out of your day.

Frank: Where am I going to find forty-five minutes? Between going to work, commuting, house maintenance, helping with the kids, I don't have time.

Hitomi: [suppressing the urge to say, "Well, I manage to do that plus more, plus work"] Would it make it easier if we worked at this together?

Frank: [not looking pleased]

Hitomi: I'm asking you sincerely, Frank, do you have any other ideas on how to make this work?

Frank: Why are you making this difficult?

Hitomi: I'm doing my best to be helpful. Can we work together instead of making this into an argument?

Frank: [a sigh and resigned nod]

Hitomi: What can we do?

Frank: I don't know.

Hitomi: Let's think about it.

It may not seem obvious on the surface, but Frank is making concessions to change. Mostly because Hitomi is coming at the conversation assertively with a balance between her needs (sharing the housework) and appreciating Frank's side (working together to integrate it into his schedule).

Maybe you're thinking this issue is never going to be resolved. It will be—just not right away. That's the thing about communication, it's all about taking baby steps together. Resolving this very large issue will take multiple attempts. Ultimately when both Hitomi and Frank have had time to think it through, they will reach and negotiate some middle ground.

How to Be an Assertive Communicator

Once you understand the basic principles of assertive communication, you can finesse your conversations by using the following techniques.

Say "I," Stop Short, and Slow Down
1. Use "I" statements.
2. Keep responses short.
3. Slow down verbally.

Your Voice, Your Body, and Your Ears
1. Monitor your tone of voice.
2. Watch non-verbal messages.
3. Listen, listen, and then listen some more.

Say "I," Stop Short, and Slow Down

1. Use "I" statements

Using "you" will automatically put your partner on the defensive—not a good thing when trying to resolve an issue. Using "I" shows you've taken responsibility for your part in this situation, and you're no longer allowing the issue to escalate to the boiling point.

2. Keep responses short

When you get into a "right fight" (e.g., a little bit of fact and tons of emotions) it shows you are trying to justify your point of view. There's no room for negotiation. By putting your feelings aside and using only the facts, your responses are short, and solutions come quickly.

3. Slow down verbally

When you start to feel out of control, you speed up the tempo of your conversation. This not only makes you uptight, but also puts your partner on edge. Show you are in control of yourself and the conversation by slowing down. This will help both you and your partner dig into the harder issues.

Your Voice, Your Body, and Your Ears

1. Monitor your tone of voice

There are dozens of ways to say "fine," and they all mean different things depending on the tone of your voice. Make sure that your tone of voice matches your words. If you're not sure, stick to how you speak to each other when you have dinner guests over.

2. Watch non-verbal messages
When people are on the defensive they unconsciously tend to go into a closed body position—arms crossed and hunched in. When your husband sees that, unconsciously he will also close up. Ensure that you have open body language and stay as relaxed as possible.

3. Listen, listen, and then listen some more
Listening is the most important thing you can do in a tough situation; however, it's usually the first thing to be tossed out the window. Listening does not mean staying quiet while coming up with your best arguments. It's about being fully present. Be careful to listen to every single word that's coming out of his mouth.

PICKING UP THE PIECES: ALSO KNOWN AS MY PARTNER IS FREAKING OUT, WHAT DO I DO?

Realistically, your first few conversations around sex won't go as you planned. You're pioneering brand-new territory and, as in any new venture, lots of mistakes will be made—a big reason couples give up. This is when you need to not only hold on to the above assertive communication but also take it up a notch.

Here's an e-mail from Liz. She wants to open a line of communication with her husband but is scared by what the conversation might turn into.

Okay, now that I understand my husband is a sensitive man with limited sex skills and training, what's next?

Am I supposed to communicate that I settled fifteen years ago for the good guy to raise kids with?

Shutting down all my own desires seems like the kindest option compared to the truth: that penetrative sex just isn't the same after three kids. Oral sex just isn't his forte. And foreplay is so time and energy consuming for little to no gain that after a full day I don't have the interest in spending hours being diddled.

Love is accepting who he is in his greatness and averageness and always having to go to sex to get an emotional connection seems a little weak at this point. Yoga is more satisfying in that regard.

How am I supposed to communicate what I want when I know it is only going to hurt him?

I'm guessing Liz has a great husband, a good marriage and, it seems, a pretty nice life. Problem is, the sexual part of the relationship no longer interests her and, I'm guessing, they've had more than a few disagreements on the topic.

Her e-mail is based on a little bit of fact: Penetration sex isn't doing it for her now and she's too tired for hours of foreplay. However, she holds back from a constructive conversation because she doesn't want to dredge up all the negative feelings she has felt for many years. Resigned and apathetic, she would prefer to "sweep it under the rug" and leave well enough alone.

Likely, the same can be said for you. You will stumble over your hurt feelings and resentment over and over again when communicating about your sex life. Don't worry. Turning your communication around is doable. The key is to take baby steps, make small victories together, and use that momentum to continue your successes.

I appreciate it's tough not to get discouraged when you go in with high hopes, and suddenly the discussion turns into the same disagreement you've been having for years. Know that this is normal. Instead of putting your tail between your legs and walking away defeated, take a deep breath and draw upon all your strength.

Before venturing into the next section, I want to stick up for your partner and give him a get-out-of-jail-free card. Even though he wants the two of you to be closer, more intimate, and have a better relationship, his logical and emotional sides will be at odds with one an-

other just like yours (you see, you two do have something in common!).
When you bring up bedroom matters, don't shame, blame, or flame him.
If he becomes a jerk, you need to give him some grace. You never know,
it may just help him manage your meltdowns more graciously.

He's Being a Complete Jerk

Although you both will be doing your best to make this situation
right—whatever form that takes—he'll inevitably slip up occasionally
and become the world's biggest jerk.

At these times you'll have two choices. You can either throw in the
towel and say, "This just isn't working," or bravely trudge on, knowing
that your brass ring is even closer because you're breaking through another
icky layer. No one likes to deal with unresolved arguments and you're no
exception. By staying the course, you're creating a very different couple
dynamic.

Allowing his jerk behaviour to go in one ear and out the other is
by no means letting him get away with his poor conduct—he probably
doesn't like being a jerk just as much as you don't like him being a jerk.
You'll get to the root of why he's acting out at some point. But for right
now, instead of holding on to your anger, resentment, and frustration
because he's being a complete jerk face, you're kindly giving him a
much-needed break; letting go of the negative feelings for the sake of
getting your sex life back on track.

For those days you want to throw your partner out with the garbage
because he is grating on your nerves (I'm certain he has to put up with
those kind of days from you too) make sure to give him a get-out-of-jail-
free card.

**YOU'RE BEING A COMPLETE JERK
GET OUT OF JAIL FREE**

Photocopy and place this card in an easily accessible place. Carry it in your wallet, or put in on your desk, fridge, or bathroom mirror. It's up to you whether you want him to see it. Then, when your partner starts to act up, you can either immediately visualize it or have it close by to remind you that this jerk phase will soon pass.

Learn from Your Disagreements

Disagreements are rotten. Yet, there's much to be learned from how you two disagree and why you disagree about specific issues. After your next fight, take a step back and analyze what happened—you're going to be stewing about it anyway, so you might as well be productive. This next section will help you figure out how things went wrong and what you can do next time to make your arguments more productive.

Handling Freak-outs Effectively

What to Expect From Him
1. Welcome the disagreement.
2. Dismiss your first gut reaction.
3. Manage your temper.
4. Sit side by side or at a 45-degree angle
5. Allow your partner to vent his feelings, and listen to him.

What Your Response Should Be
1. Repeat the main idea.
2. Ask for concrete examples.
3. Look for areas of agreement.
4. Assert yourself about how your partner is acting.
5. When all else fails, agree to disagree.

What to Expect From Him

1. Welcome the disagreement
Although you're being brave enough to initiate this conversation, understand that your partner might get defensive and disagree with

you. If your partner does start to disagree, it's your job to graciously accept his anger (as long as it's not abusive anger). Being gracious means you don't automatically tune him out; rather, you do your best to listen to why he is angry or hurting, even though you'll probably want to walk away, tell him what for, or scratch his eyes out for being insensitive.

After your first attempt at being gracious, you may experience some negative feelings toward your partner—you will feel like you're the one doing all the work. Instead, focus on being satisfied that you're creating a new, stronger, better relationship.

2. Dismiss your first gut reaction
How many times have you walked into a disagreement already keyed up because you've already rehearsed the conversation many different ways in your head? If that's what you're focusing on, that's what you'll get from the conversation. Instead, focus on what you need the result to be.

3. Manage your temper
Since you're the one instigating the discussion, it's up to you to set the tone of the conversation. Likely, you have some pent-up feelings of frustration and anxiety already. Really try to keep your negative emotions under wraps—you can work them through in future conversations. This conversation is setting the standard; it's imperative to show your partner you can have a productive conversation around sex without it turning into a disagreement.

4. Sit side by side or at a 45-degree angle
Women like to have face-to-face discussions with direct eye contact; men tend to be side by side (like when you are driving together in a car). It's best in this situation to sit side-by-side or at a 45-degree angle, because when you are face on, the direct eye contact can be offputting for you both. Side by side, both of you can say what you are really feeling.

5. Allow your partner to vent his feelings, and listen to him
You're probably sick and tired of listening to your partner whine over and over and over about the same issue. In fact, you've probably memorized his "our sex life sucks, honey" speech. It's natural that you want to tune out, start preparing your side of the argument, and wait for him to take a breath so you can tell him your side of the story.

Nevertheless, keep reminding yourself you're breaking new ground, and don't allow your eyes to glaze over. His beginning to trust you will enable better communication.

Part of the reason people avoid arguments is that they don't want to deal with their partner's mini-meltdowns. Once you graciously allow him to speak his piece, it's time to move the conversation forward.

What Your Response Should Be

1. Repeat the main idea
Deal with only one issue per marital discussion. It's hard enough sorting through one issue, never mind something your partner did ten years ago.

When you're listening to your partner, really listen to hear what he feels the problem is. You may completely disagree, but that doesn't matter. The purpose of this conversation is to work through some difficult discussions you haven't had before. If he feels it is a problem, then it is important to discuss, negotiate, and resolve.

When your partner has finished venting, pause and repeat back in your own words what you heard. It's easiest to begin your statement with, "So what I hear you saying is [fill in the blank]. Is that correct?" By using your words, you translate his situation into your level of understanding. It shows him that you were listening.

2. Ask for concrete examples
If he accuses you of something you believe is untrue, then ask him to come up with factual, specific examples of the last time you did this particular thing. Make it clear that you can understand his frustration best when he is able to give a factual example. Until he

can give you an example, there's no point in carrying on that part of the conversation.

3. Assert yourself about how your partner is acting

If you're doing your best to make this a constructive conversation and he is being cantankerous, you need to gently tell him how his actions are affecting you: "When I'm being yelled and screamed at, it makes it hard to have these discussions. I shut down and don't want to bring them up with you."

4. When all else fails, agree to disagree

Sometimes you won't find agreement. This is when you need to say you agree to disagree with your partner, and this argument can't be used against each other in the future.

Just because you cannot resolve an issue at one sitting doesn't mean it won't ever be resolved. You've now set the stage for productive communication even when it becomes difficult.

What If He Refuses to Communicate?

Determine why he won't talk to you. Is it that he can't or he simply won't? Most of the time, your partner doesn't know how to communicate or he's tried, made a real mess of things, and didn't like looking foolish. So it's up to you to determine why the communication's stalled. My bet is that he's scared.

Most likely your guy has been socialized in a completely different way than you when it comes to conversations around sex. Bravado in the locker room is sometimes the only opportunity he's had to talk about sex. With this in mind, try to appreciate that it's incredibly hard for him to suddenly turn this around and instantly articulate his deepest feelings.

Give him time. We all need a chance to collect our thoughts and sort them out—and some of us need more time than others. He may not be able to communicate on your timeline. Analytical partners, particularly, need time to formulate their thoughts.

Give him space, which will create a more relaxed atmosphere. People make better and quicker decisions when they're relaxed.

Build trust. Are you doing everything you can so that he feels safe opening up and having a meaningful conversation? If he's still not talking after a few weeks, ask yourself these questions:

- Is your conduct erratic? One minute you're calm and then the next you're angry for no "apparent" reason. Perhaps his experience of having these conversations with you has been less than appealing. He needs to see and trust that you won't behave in that old, ineffective way.
- Do you treat promises lightly? Do try to get him to talk by promising you won't freak out if he tells you, only to turn around and freak out once he does tell you?
- Is what you communicate deceptive or dishonest? Do you have a hidden agenda for this conversation? Are you trying to manipulate things to your way of thinking? You may say no, but many times, unconsciously, that's what's happening. Be clear to yourself and him what your motives are.

If your partner has learned that the best way to avoid an argument is by not communicating, then he needs gentle reinforcement. Approach cautiously. Charging into the conversation (even if your best intentions are to fix the problem) won't motivate him to come out of his shell. He may need a little coaxing.

WRAP-UP

You likely don't communicate your sexual wants, needs, and desires to your partner because you're afraid of his reaction. Both of you have probably tried to talk to each other about your sex life, and one or both of you quickly got upset. No one wants to put themselves in a position where they know their partner is going to have a mini-meltdown.

If you're serious about helping your situation, going in prepared will help both you and your partner walk away with solutions rather than hard feelings.

It's time to bring up the topic of what you want out of the sexual experience. To do that you need to know what you want and then set a goal to get there.

KEY POINTS

1. Great sex is all about great communication.
2. Pick one idea that will improve communication between you and your partner, put it into practice, and become comfortable with it before moving on.
3. Good communication habits involve baby steps.
4. Assertive communication means you both walk away winners.
5. Learn from your arguments and learn to negotiate a win/win.

CHAPTER 5

Creating the Sex Life That You Want

"Most couples make the mistake of giving each other the 'remains of the day'—the leftover time after every other relationship and task has been attended to. This is not only backwards, but destructive. How many relationships have been damaged, or even destroyed, by engaging in difficult conversations that deeply affect the relationship when partners are tired, stressed, rushed, and irritated at the end of the day? Stellar partners give each other *prime time* and make each other their *top priority*. All good flows from there."

—Rhoberta Shaler, Ph.D.

WHAT DO YOU WANT YOUR SEX LIFE TO BE?

To begin any journey you need a road map. So before you begin your venture into married-woman sex, you'd better have a good idea of how you're going to get there. At the very least, you need to plant ideas in your brain so your subconscious can eventually come up with a solution.

Bottom line: If you don't have a plan of how you want to get your sex life back on track, chances are you won't succeed.

Your sex goals should be much bigger than simply getting out of your uncomfortable single-woman-sex mess. The goals should turn your focus away from what you don't want and to concentrate on what you *do* want. You need to use your goals to build a solid sex foundation. You need to ask yourself what you want your sex life to be, realistically, six months from now, a year from now, twenty years from now.

It Starts with Knowing What You Want

Telling me what you don't like or don't want in your sex life is easy. The more important question is, what do you want your sex life to be? When I ask women this question in seminars, they usually give me a blank stare. I'm certain they're thinking, "Um, that's why I'm here. So you can tell me." Perhaps you're thinking the same thing. You've got to figure this out yourself.

Here are a few ideas to put your brain in gear.

One woman said sex would be better if there was a lot more cuddle time. Another said she wanted a "minute" before sex to connect so she could have a "moment" during sex with her partner. Another woman had recently gone through menopause and said she wanted her partner to treat her body differently. When I asked what was stopping her from telling him, sheepishly she admitted it was herself. Another explained good sex for her would be to take a bath with her partner. When she got out of the bath she didn't want to have intercourse; she simply wanted to share that time with her partner.

Something to note: When I give these examples in workshops, men are generally befuddled. They do not understand how a cuddle, a minute, communication, or a bath is a sexual experience (because, quite frankly, for them it isn't). Men (and women) assume sex equals intercourse. Your definition around what makes up a sexual experience needs to become very broad.

What the above women desire is intimacy. They may or may not want intercourse, but it seems none of them want the pressure associated with having to have intercourse. Instead, they want the attention and care that comes from being intimate. Remember, emancipation tells us that your sexual needs, desires, and wants are equal in importance to his.

Chances are what you want in your sexual experience is to have shared intimacy. Let your partner know that improved intimacy will increase your sexual desire and, we hope, your sexual arousal—which may mean you want sex more often. Everyone wins.

What Is a Goal?

No doubt you've heard about goals. It's exciting to think that you really can change some things about your life that you don't like: get out of credit card debt, go on vacation somewhere tropical, quit smoking, lose a few pounds.

Goals are positive dreams you want to create for your life; they give hope for a better, bigger, brighter life. However, goals don't become real until you take decisive action. (For example, many couples have inadvertently created a sex goal by making sex happen at least once a week.) Creating goals gives you purpose and reason while you're working through your sexual baggage because the goal keeps your eye on the prize: married-woman sex.

Taking a Big Idea and Breaking It into Doable Chunks

Successfully working toward the big goal of having lifelong married-woman sex means breaking that big goal into smaller chunks. Otherwise your brain will quickly become overloaded with how to make it happen, and have you abandon your goal long before you ever really get started. So here's a breakdown of how to make your big goal work within the context of your busy life.

Big goals are meant to be big-picture thinking. It's what you want to have happen over the next one to twenty years (e.g., to improve your health through exercise). There is no instant gratification; rather, a commitment to change something over the long term.

Small goals are what you want to have happen in the foreseeable future, two weeks to six months (such as get into the routine of walking four times a week). They are stepping stones that reap small victories to keep you motivated as you work your way toward your big goal.

Tasks are you putting your small goal into action (such as buying a proper pair of outdoor walking shoes). Whereas goals are the ideas, tasks make the ideas a reality.

The sequence goes like this:

Big goal	=	A lifetime of married-woman sex
Small goal	=	Make your partner a priority
Task	=	Create daily affectionate touch

Here are some other things to consider when creating your goals:

- Be specific. The more specific you can be about what you want your sex life to be, the easier it will be for you to achieve.
- Be logical. Whereas the right brain (or emotional and creative side), comes up with the idea for your goal, it's the left brain (or the logical side) that will put your goals into action. The more factual and concrete you can be with your goals, the easier it will be for your left side to kick itself into high gear.
- Make it attainable. Every good goal will push you a little outside your comfort zone; however, it still needs to fit into the context of your daily life.
- Set a timeframe. By setting a schedule and sticking to it, the left side of your brain will inevitably get you to your goal before you expected.

The rest of this book will show you how to make new sex habits easy by creating tasks for each small goal.

As a multi-tasking guru, you might believe that small goals and tasks aren't making you work hard enough and you could be doing more. Trust me, working through a small goal, like daily affectionate touching, will prove to be a worthy effort.

So, even if you aren't trying to sabotage your efforts, you may end up shooting yourself in the foot by trying to turn your sex life around in six months or less. Granted, there are people who can and do. For the rest of us, consider how long you've been with your partner; the longer you've been creating poor habits, the longer it will take to create positive habits. As well, consider how much time you have to spare toward your goal. If you can focus a lot of time and energy on your goal, six months is realistic; if not, you'll be looking at least one year before you see any tangible results.

Vague Goals versus Achievable Goals

Here are four examples of changing vague goals to achievable goals that your left brain can wrap itself around. Notice each achievable goal has both a small goal and a task.

1. Vague goal: I want more romance.
   Achievable goal: To have more romance, for the next year we will have one date night per month; we will alternate who takes responsibility for setting up the date night.

2. Vague goal: I want us to be closer.
   Achievable goal: To bring us closer, I've hung a smoochie picture of us on the refrigerator to remind me of good times, and I will kiss or hug my partner every day for the next six months.

3. Vague goal: I want our sex life to be happier.
   Achievable goal: I want us to affectionately touch each other at least once per day.

4. Vague goal: I want us to stop disagreeing about sex.
   Achievable goal: I want to have a more positive energy between us. Every day for the next three months I will look for things my partner is doing right and make sure to tell him

before I go to sleep. (Notice the language goes from negative "stop disagreeing" to affirmative "positive energy.")

Don't Do It Alone

It's best to get buy-in from your partner. However, if you decide to create a goal and not tell your partner what you're up to (shame, shame, shame), then expect that you'll be doing all the work and feeling resentment for trying to make your relationship work. Simply by letting him know what you are up to will set the process off on the right foot.

Be Realistic About the Sex Outcome

Although creating a new sex life is rejuvenating to a sex life, it doesn't mean your sexual experience will always be a slam dunk. With the ebb and flow of life, every sexual encounter will range from mind blowing to (yes, it's true) terrible. Barry and Emily McCarthy's book, *Rekindling Desire*, give these statistics:

40 to 50 per cent will be mutually satisfying

20 to 25 per cent will be good for one spouse and okay for the other

20 to 25 per cent will be good for one spouse with the other going along

5 to 15 per cent will have mediocre, unsatisfying or even be failures

Self-Esteem Sabotage

Be aware of any sabotaging you may unconsciously try to do. Your self-esteem may dictate that you don't deserve to have dreams. But you *do* deserve to have a happy, healthy, and fulfilling sex life. If you're having a hard time starting to set your goals, it may indicate that your self-esteem needs a little work.

What You Will Experience While Working through Your Goal

Now that you know how to set an achievable goal, you need to know what you will experience as you work toward it. Achieving your goal will involve a series of steps. Knowing where you're at in the series will help move you forward especially when the motivation has dwindled.

The Honeymoon Phase

Out of the gate, you get your first hit of goal adrenaline. With zeal and newfound hope, the first week is a snap; you can't believe you didn't do this sooner. You come in with a great attitude and you have the world at your feet. It's such a rush to know you can accomplish what you've set your mind to.

Willpower Hump

After the initial adrenaline rush, you're left with only your willpower. By the second or third week, your motivation starts to wane and life's little hiccups occur, "forcing" you to create excuses about why you can't be as eager as you were the week before. Procrastination begins. Simultaneous self-sabotage has you believing you don't deserve this happiness.

This is a crucial point where most people give up. You must steel yourself to keep on track. Keep your big goal in mind: married-woman sex and a lifetime of happy intimacy.

Celebrate Your Accomplishment

Even if there isn't a marching band to announce your accomplishment, it's important for you to celebrate completing small goals or tasks such as looking for and saying positive things to your partner every day. Give yourself a pat on the back, e-mail your partner to say, "We did it!" Make sure to acknowledge your achievement. Positive reinforcement will help both of you take on the next task.

Creating a goal together, working toward it, and accomplishing the tasks will ultimately bring you and your partner closer. It doesn't get much better than that. However, your goals will never manifest themselves unless they are in alignment with your priorities. Your priorities must be in alignment with your goals; otherwise you will have only a great plan—with zero follow-through. Next we'll see if what you want matches up with what you value.

PRIORITY CHECK-IN

As a busy woman, every day you have a thousand things vying for your attention. Have you every asked yourself Do I choose my priorities or do my priorities choose me? Where you spend your time becomes what you value; what you value becomes what you prioritize; what you prioritize comprises your day-to-day routine.

To achieve married-woman sex it's imperative to value your need for intimacy, equality, and bodily pleasure. Therefore, in your day-to-day routine, you need to create one-on-one time and make your partner a priority. To be sure, this is challenging. Many women already cut back on sleep, don't have a lot of extra time, and are going as fast as they can to just keep up. Too many are unfairly hard on themselves and wonder why they can't do more or achieve what other women seem to.

Consequently, you must take a good hard look at your priorities and decide which are serving you and which are working against your goal. Watch out: This is where small-goal paralysis takes over and excuses start flying around. Be aware of any "yeah buts": "Yeah, I know it's really important to make my partner a priority but [insert excuse here]."

To achieve your big and small goals, you will have to take a step back and refocus on what really matters to you: looking good for everyone else (and not having time for your partner); or having a fun and meaningful sex life (and loosening the perfectionist reins).

Martyrdom Factor

You're fighting another strongly ingrained belief, or meme: martyrdom. Society reveres women who selflessly gave it all up for the "good" of others. But you *can* be a good woman and have time for yourself.

The battle to find "me time" is ongoing. Time management and balance experts state that the best way to manage everything going on in your life is to give yourself much-needed time and space so you can decompress and recharge your batteries. But wanting to be seen as a "good woman" by raising good children, being an excellent employee, keeping a clean house, and being a good cook, seems to take over. You really want to make yourself a priority; you just don't know how to fit it into your already overflowing schedule.

It comes down to choice. Bottom line: In order to have a great sex life, you need to make you, your relationship, and your sexual needs a priority. Here's the kicker: When you do have a happy, healthy relationship, other parts of your life improve.

Your Top Five Priorities

To start, write down your top five priorities in your personal and professional life. Did you list yourself as one of your top five priorities? Did you list your kids and then get stuck? Maybe you listed what you would *like* to be your top five priorities? That is, perhaps you put your spouse in the top five; however, when it comes to follow-through, your words and actions wouldn't support that.

A big part of making your partnership a priority is following through with what you're saying. It's not enough to say that from now on you're going to make yourself a priority. You must show it in concrete actions.

Why Is It Hard to Switch Priorities?

Priorities are built upon a myriad of small daily habits. When shifting your priorities, it means changing something in your already established and comfortable routine. Making the tiniest change may create a domino effect on the sequence of events. Feeling overwhelmed during this time of change is perfectly normal because you're not only changing things; you're rearranging a cluster of tried-and-true techniques that help you get through the day.

This is why having doable tasks is so very important. Instead of becoming overwhelmed by how much change needs to take place, focus on one task. Once you easily fit it into your daily routine, incorporate the next task. It's truly a recipe for success.

Let's Work on Making Sex a Priority

Getting your sex life back on track means taking a look at what you truly value, and no longer coasting and hoping for the best. Here are some things to think about.

- List your top five priorities.
- What are your top three time wasters? How can you stop yourself from spending so much wasted time?
- What could you do to carve out ten minutes a day to spend some quality one-on-one time with your partner?
- Do your words support your actions? Are you saying you want a better sex life but your actions mean that you avoid intimacy?
- What are some of the things that would have to happen before putting your sex life back on your priority list?

TWO PERSONALITY TYPES HAVING ONE TYPE OF SEX

As sex is a team sport, you must value your partner's priorities as much as your own. Understanding why your partner interacts and communicates the way he does—his personality style–can make all the difference when it comes to creating a new sex life.

Most likely, you've married your opposite in personality style. Based on professional and personal experience, I've come to the conclusion that we marry our opposite for basic survival purposes. Your hard-wiring is attracted to those people with qualities you lack, thereby creating a completed "unit" with the ability to take on and survive most of life's complications.

Ironically, what you need and value in your mate is also what drives you crazy in and outside the bedroom. The difference in how you see the world and the variations in your communication styles can wreak havoc on getting your sex life back on track.

The couples who fail miserably at sexual resolution are forever trying to force their partner to understand things from their perspective. Instead, it's valuable to understand and appreciate how your partner thinks, feels, and reacts. Once you understand your partner's perspective it will become infinitely easier to negotiate your new and exciting bedroom goal. To do this, we'll focus on personality styles.

Determining Your Partner's Personality Style

The study of personality styles can be quite complex, but for the purposes of this book we will simplify the Myers-Briggs personality test.

Myers-Briggs Variables

In the 1930s, mother–daughter team Katherine Briggs and Isabel Myers devised a personality test incorporating some of Carl Jung's ideas. Myers-Briggs tests for four major groups: introvert versus extrovert, sensing versus intuition, thinking versus feeling, and judging versus perceiving

It's important to note that all personality types tend to be one personality style at work and another at home. You need to think about and focus on how you behave while at home with your partner.

Introvert versus Extrovert

Where You Get Your Energy

Introverts tend to get their energy from being by themselves: reading, gardening, jogging. Too much commotion sucks the life right out of them.

Extroverts tend to get their energy from being around other people: team sports, volunteer work, going to parties. Being by themselves for too long sucks the life right out of them.

If you're uncertain whether you're an introvert or extrovert, consider what you do when you're under stress. An introvert will find a way to be alone; an extrovert will seek out the comfort and attention of other people.

Where Introverts and Extroverts Clash

Let's say you're an extrovert. You've had a long, stressful day and what you want most when you get home is to connect with your hubby by talking. Your partner, who is an introvert and has also had a rotten day, walks through the door, nods in your direction, goes directly to the newspaper/television/computer, and becomes engrossed.

You try to engage him in conversation but he just gives a warning grunt, which means he'll get snappy if you don't stop. Come bedtime, hubby has had a few alone hours to recharge his batteries, while your batteries still need an extrovert boost. Guess how much sex you'll want to have versus your partner who's got his energy back?

Sensing versus Intuition
How You and Your Partner Process Data
Sensing people focus on the here and now and are concrete thinkers. They prefer to use one of their five senses to receive data. Intuitive people focus on the big picture, think in future terms, and see patterns and possibilities. They receive their data from their subconscious or insights.

Where Sensing and Intuitive People Clash
This is an especially tricky one when working through a difficult bedroom situation. A sensing person will, most likely, be able to see how the relationship has gone sideways, and focus goal-setting ideas on the present. The intuitive person will constantly be focused on and setting goals for what the future relationship could be instead of what it currently is.

It's hard for a sensing person to understand the intuitive person's dreams and schemes, and the intuitive person can't understand why the sensing person is stuck in the present.

Thinking versus Feeling
How You Make a Decision
Thinkers decide with their heads and base their decisions on logic. Feelers make decisions with their hearts, basing their decisions on values or person-centred concerns.

Where Thinkers and Feelers Clash

When creating goals, thinkers want concrete benchmarks to show they have met the goal (e.g., of having sex once a week). However, feelers will create emotional goals like having more closeness between the two of you. You need to combine these two aspects by creating a goal like: We will become closer by sitting down and talking one-on-one with no distractions for at least five minutes every day for the rest of your marriage.

Judging versus Perceiving

How You Deal with the World at Large

Judging people (which has nothing to do with being judgmental of others) like to be organized and have a plan. They like things to be figured out and settled before the day even begins.

Perceivers (which does not refer to whether or not someone is perceptive) are more flexible and spontaneous with time, preferring to keep their options open.

Where Judging and Perceivers Clash

A judging personality has figured out her day and suddenly her perceptive partner gives them a nudge for a little nookie—it's irritating to her because she hasn't allowed for it in her schedule. A judging personality would think it a very good goal to schedule a date night, sex, and/or time spent alone together. A perceiver, however, is almost offended by the idea that sex and intimacy has to be scheduled and cannot happen spontaneously.

Creating a solid sexual future takes the work of two people, so it's critical to enlist your partner. Knowing how his personality, goals, and priorities differ from yours means that you can work together to decide on goals and execute them.

KEY POINTS

1. To begin any journey you must know where you are going. Setting goals in your sex life is the easiest way for you and your partner to create a plan of how to get your sex life back on track.

2. You need to value and prioritize shared time with your partner..

3. There are four basic personality styles. People usually partner with their opposite personality style, then don't know why they can't figure out their partner. Understanding your partner's differences will enable you both to move forward in creating a new sex life.

CHAPTER 6

Your Sexual Needs Are Equal

"Sexuality is a powerful window into who we are."

—David Schnarch, Ph.D., *Passionate Marriage*

Now that you've sorted through your baggage, got the communication flowing and determined what good sex means to you, it's time to move into having married-woman sex. Hooray!

In the next few pages you will find out how to craft a sexual experience where intimacy, nurturing, and being cared for are the name of your married-woman-sex game.

The best way to both get you started and to ease you and your partner into this new sexual groove is by creating good intimacy habits outside the bedroom. Not only will these new habits boost your sexual self-confidence, they will also raise your day-to-day desire to have sex. Once you've mastered great intimacy outside the bedroom, it will be a snap to raise your needs, follow through on your terms, and not feel guilty enjoying yourself inside the bedroom (discussed in Chapter 8).

GREAT SEX IS FRAGILE

It takes twenty-eight days to form a habit. What, in the next twenty-eight days, do you need to have so that your brain starts to rewire itself into healthier sex habits?

Positive sex habits outside the bedroom will help you keep the momentum going even when experiencing life's up and downs. In essence, they create a firewall around your long-term married-woman sex. Don't fool yourself: Great sex, intimacy, and a deep emotional connection are fragile. However, keeping this excitement and momentum over the long term is certainly doable; it's simply a matter of not allowing your most important relationship to go back to cruise control.

The usual feedback I hear from couples in the process of upgrading their sex is, "We were doing so well and then something happened. Life got in the way and we lost our momentum." Your first knee-jerk emotional reaction to a difficult situation will determine your sexual destiny. It makes sense, then, that when you have established good intimacy habits outside the bedroom, your sex won't have the dramatic ups and downs resulting from the ebb and flow of life. Therefore, this chapter provides many easy-to-achieve good practices, which you can make into habits, to keep you on track.

It is exciting to know that a lifelong love affair with your special someone is within your grasp? Sex can again be a fun and meaningful part of your relationship—instead of the enemy!

YOUR FIVE-MINUTES-A-DAY FUSS LIST

Now that you've moved your mate and your marriage up on the priority list, we need to put you up there too.

Making yourself a priority outside the bedroom is the first step to making yourself a priority inside the bedroom. You're probably low woman on the totem pole for pretty much everything in your life: your kids come first, your boss tells you what to do, you don't ever say what you want in the bedroom.

Massaging Women

To emphasize how hard it is for women to make themselves a priority, at seminars I sometimes ask women to get into groups of four. I assign an exercise in which three women (non-sexually) massage the other woman; each woman gets a turn being massaged. The woman who's being massaged has three tasks: (1) experience how good it feels to have other people fuss all over her; (2) tell the other three women strategically placed at her head, body, and legs how she wants to be massaged; and (3) give feedback to say if the three women's massaging techniques are exactly what she wants to experience or if they're too hard or too soft.

Every single time we've done this exercise, the woman being massaged can't tell the others what she wants. She takes what she is given—unless a massaging technique becomes too uncomfortable to bear. In which case her feedback is, "I'm sorry to bug you. You're doing a great job. It's just that, well, my neck's a little sensitive and if you didn't mind too much, it would be great if you could be a little more gentle." She'll go to great lengths not to hurt the other women's feelings.

After this exercise, the feedback has consistently been a feeling of overwhelming guilt. The women knew they should enjoy the massage but aren't used to being pampered. They liked their massages but knew if they had given some feedback, they'd have enjoyed their massages even more. They felt frustrated, and didn't know how to verbalize their wants. Plus, the entire time, they couldn't totally relax because they felt they should in some way be reciprocating.

This small but powerful exercise reflects a massive problem in the bedroom. Women want their sex life to be different. Yet when it comes time to say to their partner, "I need as much pleasure out of this sexual experience as you. We need to start having married-woman sex," they are stopped dead in their tracks because they can't make themselves a priority. (Remember the third component to single-woman sex is the man is the priority in the bedroom.)

It's Time to Be Your Priority

Everyone in your life will win when you start making yourself a priority. You'll feel better about yourself, your self-esteem will grow, and you'll be a nicer person to be around. Treating yourself well is a recipe for success. And it doesn't have to take a lot of time and effort. You simply put yourself on the top-five priority list and follow through with what you've said.

Your Daily Fuss List

Be fussy. This means paying attention and awakening your five senses: touch, sight, hearing, taste, and smell. The bonus is that you're also awakening your sexual desire. Here are some ideas you can implement immediately:

- Feel the bubbles of soap caress your body as you wash yourself in the shower or bath.
- Pluck your eyebrows.
- Take time to carefully massage lotion into your hands, particularly between the fingers.
- Have a once-a-day, non-guilty indulgence of your favourite treat.
- Call a friend you haven't spoken to in a long time.
- Stroll by the perfume counter and try a new fragrance.
- While driving, if you hear your favourite song, keep it on even though other people in the car might not appreciate your musical taste.
- Determine your favourite passion—surprisingly too many women can't say what stirs the fires of passion in their belly.
- Indulge in something you want to do, like lying in bed and reading a magazine, and don't feel guilty letting the housework sit for one night.
- Take a bath with fancy bath salts, lotions, and potions. Soak, read a book, and relax.
- Look through magazines to see if there's a new hairstyle you want to try.

- Talk to your partner about having a minimum one night off per month.
- Try a new food at the supermarket or while out for lunch.
- Give yourself a facial.
- Give yourself a pedicure.
- Give yourself a manicure.
- Exfoliate your legs while in the shower.
- Give yourself a head massage while washing your hair.
- Really taste your food while you're eating your lunch or any other time you rush your meal.
- Smile at a stranger.
- Smile at your partner.

There are so many other ways to treat yourself; the point is, every day do something for yourself, *only for yourself*. Start believing how important it is to be one of your top five priorities. The more you can make this happen, the easier it will be for you to slide into creating a satisfying space for sex.

THE GIFT OF TOUCH

GOOD IDEA:
Every day touch your partner affectionately.

Before my husband and I got our sex life back on track, I was telling a friend how it irked me that as soon as I started to do housework, my husband would become affectionate with me. Exasperated, I explained, "It's like he has a Martha Stewart sex fetish or something. Can't he see I'm in the middle of something and he's seriously getting in my way?" My friend looked genuinely shocked and replied, "Really?

My favourite thing is when my husband comes and starts touching me when I'm in the middle of a mundane chore. It makes the chore that much more pleasurable."

It was my turn to be shocked. There I was expecting united married-woman sympathy, and she turned my argument on its head. I'm happy to report that her comment was a key turning point to my sexual happiness. Instead of affectionate touch being an "Oh great, he wants sex" nuisance, it will help ease you into the sexual experience. You see, for many women sexual desire is triggered by touch. During foreplay, your skin sends signals to your brain, which responds by flooding your brain with the hormone oxytocin. Ongoing, daily affectionate touch is a cornerstone to having a satisfying and active sex life.

How Did Your Touch Become Almost Nonexistent?

How can you tell a brand-new couple? They're wrapped around each other, and can't be separated without feeling some touch-loss anxiety. They glow with all those wonderful feelings of needing and wanting, and are grateful to be near and to touch this person they're so darn attracted to. It has nothing to do with needy or clingy and everything to do with all the feel-good hormones propelling the couple to touch. Being so tactile means sexual contact and connection is always a heartbeat away.

After the first year, the couple feels comfortable in the relationship, and doesn't feel the need to touch as much. After year two, when the love drugs have worn off, the shift in touching sensibility is visible. Couples are still affectionate, still hug and give chaste kisses, but that urgent sense of non-sexual, need-to-be-near-you touching has ceased. At this point, four things put touch on the back burner: a shift in priorities, being touched out, a lack of good feelings, and diminished sexual self-confidence.

Shift in Priorities

Because you felt secure in this relationship, you felt safe shifting your mate from the top of your priorities to below everything else. In doing so, touch became less important.

Being Touched Out

Many women with small children feel touched-out from breast-feeding, being pulled, holding babies and children.

Lack of Good Feelings

The lack of good feelings directly coincides with moving into Stage 2 of a relationship—where instead of seeing everything right about your partner (Stage 1), you start to find everything wrong about him (see page 43). Not surprisingly, when you start picking out his flaws and he starts picking out yours, you really don't want to touch him. You begin to rebuff his touch, and as the picking gets worse, the more turned off touch you become.

Diminished Sexual Self-Confidence

If you are one of the 80 per cent of women who don't like their body, you are probably self-conscious about its "flaws" and therefore less willing to show it off and have it touched. Again, you become disconnected from your partner.

Your Turn for Touch

Women need to have a connection "minute" before sex so they can have a connected "moment" during sex. The sad irony is that many women come to associate being touched by their partner as the initiation into sex: "Oh great, he's massaging my neck/kissing my cheek/trying to cuddle me . . . it must mean he wants sex now." Soon you believe he offers affectionate touch only when he wants to get a little something. Which may or may not be true.

Touching and being touched by your partner every day is a surefire way for a woman to already feel connected to her partner before they hit the sheets. To turn your situation around, start welcoming touch back into your daily routine. In fact, actively pursue it. The rewards you'll reap are huge.

Touch Test

This is a good barometer to see where the touch is in your relationship.

1. How often do you and your partner affectionately touch each other?
2. What is your gut reaction when your partner touches you?
3. How much touch do you feel comfortable with?
4. What would it take to touch your partner every day?

Every day without exception, look for ways to playfully touch your partner. Hug him, squeeze his butt (my personal favourite), hold his hand (when was the last time you walked down the street hand in hand with your man?), or give him a peck on the cheek. Anything that non-verbally says to your partner, "I like you, I'm thinking about you, and I want you to know how much you mean to me."

Natasha and her husband have their "ten-second kiss." When things are getting too hectic in their household or they start snapping at each other, she or her husband will suddenly yell out, "ten-second kiss." Everything gets dropped and they kiss for ten seconds. What she likes about this kiss is that sex plays no part; it's simply a reconnection kiss. Julie and her husband have a similar good habit but with a "ten-second hug." Besides bringing up all the feel-good hormones in her body, it instantly connects Julie to her partner.

Freeze, Chill, and Lean

You also need to be comfortable with him touching you. If you tense up as soon as he touches you, you need to "freeze" that behaviour as it happens. In other words, catch yourself and don't rebuff his touch.

Once you learn to freeze your behaviour, you must then make a conscious effort to "chill"—tell yourself that your partner doesn't necessarily want sex from you. Okay, to be fair, when you first start doing this he probably does want sex, but he probably doesn't know any other way to initiate, so you need to just "chill" with it for the time being. Allow your body to feel his touch instead of shutting down all feel-good circuits; at the same time, forbid your brain to start the old and familiar rant of, "You want sex now? Can't you see I'm tired/busy?"

It will take a while before you get used to being touched. How long depends on the amount of time you've been together and how long you've been rebuffing his touch. A realistic timeline is three to six months.

Once you're okay with chilling when he touches you, it's time to "lean" into his touch. Allow yourself to feel pleasurable touch that isn't associated with sex. Let him give your tired shoulders a mini-massage without feeling guilty, and without having to massage his shoulders in return. Lean into his touch and allow your body to feel the warmth and love from your partner.

Once you're in the freeze, chill, and lean mode, you will see a difference in your ability to get into sex because your body is used to him touching you. His touch is no longer associated with resentful feelings, so you don't have to switch your brain off and turn your body on. The constant, affectionate touch between the two of you has your body halfway there.

MAKE YOUR PARTNER RIGHT

> **GOOD IDEA:**
> Every day look for and acknowledge what
> your partner did right rather than the things he
> might have done wrong.

Couples who have long-term marital success find more things right about their partner than wrong. That makes sense. When you acknowledge and show love toward your partner, he's going to feel better about himself and, hopefully, reciprocate.

Make Him Right Every Day

During this time, look for the subtle things he does to help, instead of looking for the ways he doesn't. Every day, without exception—yes, even when he's being a complete jerk—you need to look for and find at least one thing he's done right. It could be as simple as, "Thank you for taking out the garbage." Now, we both know there's really no reason you should be thanking him for something that is his job—he certainly doesn't thank you for the ten thousand things you do in a day. However, don't go to bed until you've praised your partner. Here are some ideas:

- Is he a good parent?
- Does he like to cook?
- Does he clean up?
- Does he take care of his appearance (i.e., wears cologne)?
- Does he work well on big projects (such as renovating a house)?
- Is he good in a crisis?
- Does he get along with your family?
- Does he enjoy entertaining?
- Is he fun on vacation?

Every day is filled with him doing good things; find a few and praise him for them.

What Gets Recognized Gets Repeated

Let this be your mantra: Focus on his results rather than his process.

It's basic human nature to want positive reinforcement. As long as you see efforts being made on his end, heap on the praise for any effort—big or small. Why should you be so gracious and giving? When you take the time to notice him doing something good and comment on it, he will be more likely to repeat the positive behaviour. If you don't notice or take the time to praise he will be more inclined to give up and revert to his old familiar patterns, frustrated by the process.

Don't get bent out of shape if he doesn't notice your efforts or return the praise—even though you absolutely deserve it. Please take heart and do not become discouraged.

Why It's Important to Acknowledge
1. People feel their partner exaggerates what is sexually wrong. Looking for strengths enables both partners to feel affirmed and they'll have more trust in the change process.
2. Change means scary feelings are dredged up and a scary situation can look hopeless. Looking at the bright side eases you from hopelessness to optimism.

Being Nice to Your Partner Is the Only Option

It is critical to continue your positive momentum so you can create positive changes in your relationship.

When you first start to recognize the good he's done, he might think, "What does she want?" After a week though, still confused, he'll probably mumble, "Thanks" or "You're welcome." Pretty soon, when he sees that your comments are not sarcastic and you have no agenda, he'll look forward to hearing them.

Good energy cannot help but produce good energy. Although weak at the start, it'll strengthen if you keep the momentum going. Commit to praising. Your goal is to keep it going every single day for the rest of your life.

GOOD IDEA:
Make him feel good even when you are
ticked off at him. In fact, this is the best time:
It will turn your thinking around and perhaps
stop an unnecessary disagreement. I realize
this may seem difficult. Give his hand a
squeeze and say, "I appreciate how hard you're
working." The touch and the encouraging words
will shift the momentum from angry to you two
once again working together.

The Five-to-One Rule

Once you get into the groove of making him right every day, it's time
to kick it up a notch. You need to figure out the ratio of how many
times you criticize him versus how many times you compliment him.
Ultimately you want to build up to every time you make him wrong,
you find five ways to make him right. If you think this is an overwhelming task, you should ask yourself why it's so easy for you to make
him feel bad and so hard to make him feel good.

A VISION OF SEX LOVELINESS

I hang around with motivational-speaker types and for years they've
raved about vision boards. Using the idea that "a picture's worth a thousand words," a vision board is a bulletin board comprising images of
what you want your life to be.

For many years I shied away from vision boards. It's not that I didn't
believe in them (okay, truth be known, inwardly I sat smug thinking I
was above making a vision board), I just: didn't have the time; didn't
think it was necessary; didn't want people to think I needed a vision
board; fill in all the other excuses here. That is until one of my mentors

"encouraged" me to do one. Well, guess what? Vision boards really do work and have an enormous impact on rewiring your brain.

When my marriage was at its worst, I created a vision board of magazine pictures showing happy couples in intimate poses. For the next few months, whenever my husband and I had a fight, and I thought, "He's completely ticking me off; why am I in this relationship?" I would look at the photos to remind myself of what I wanted our marriage to eventually be.

Seeing the vision board immediately took me out of my victim-think and put me back in the driver's seat of what I want my relationship to be. The relationship mess I was currently experiencing didn't instantly clear up; however, I went back and communicated through the situation assertively. The vision board turned out to be a big part of bringing intimacy back into my relationship.

Your Vision Board

To create your own vision board, you need to collect visual reminders: an old photo of you two happily in love; a picture from a magazine of a couple you want to emulate; something you've written down; an article you've clipped from a magazine; a photo that created a positive emotional reaction.

When you're having a rough time or disagreeing with your partner, seek out your vision board to remind yourself of your goal. It will become your lifeline.

What Will Be Your Reminders?

I appreciate you may find the vision board corny—I did before I tried it. If you don't use this idea, create some other image of what you want your relationship and sex life to be. That is, when things start to go sideways, have something concrete that you can focus on instead of stewing about what's going wrong.

DO YOU SELL YOURSELF TO YOUR PARTNER OR DOES HE WANT A REFUND?

GOOD IDEA:
Find ways to treat your partner with kindness and romantic gestures that makes him feel special.

Romantic gestures show that you and your partner take care of one another. Both of you need to show kind gestures to one another to build up your bedroom intimacy.

A reporter asked me to do an interview about nice things someone could do for a spouse. When we first spoke to set up an interview time, she explained, "I need specific, concrete ideas. For example, one lady makes sure to have a warm towel from the dryer ready for her husband when he steps out of the shower." Wow! I imagined how exquisite it would be to have my husband wrap me up in a warm towel right after a shower. It wasn't even so much a warm towel, it was the caring gesture.

For the next four days, before the scheduled interview, I wracked my brain. It was a Catch-22, because although there are hundreds of nice things you can do for your mate, they aren't necessarily practical. Being wrapped in a towel when you get out of the shower is a great idea, but how likely would it be for the average busy woman to have the time to follow through? Continue reading for suggestions that you'll find easy to incorporate in your daily routine.

Women really dig romance—and it easily leads to intimacy. Win-win! To get your sex life back on track, every day you need to "sell" yourself to your partner. By selling I mean taking care of yourself, your partner, and your relationship. When couples stop selling, one or both will want a refund.

Why Does Romance Die?

We let our relationship slide when we become lazy in making our partners feel special with excuses like, I don't have the time, the energy, the money, the creativity, or whatever. When romance declines, confusion and frustration grow as sexual interest wanes. Both men and women feel betrayed that they were sold the wrong bill of goods, "This person used to shower me in all kinds of loving attention. Now, nothing. Am I valued at all?"

So if everything about romance is so wonderful, why did it stop? You need to ask yourself why you stopped going out of your way to do thoughtful things for your partner—especially since it made you feel good to make your guy feel special, and he enjoyed it so much.

Here are some ideas for introducing romance back into your relationship:

1. Write a list of things you find romantic and ask your husband to do the same. Encourage each other to pull out the list and occasionally do something from it as a surprise.
2. Take turns planning romantic evenings or weekends together. Marking them on the calendar helps both individuals remember.
3. Leave a love note, love voice mail, or love e-mail.
4. Start up and never stop going on dates. Movies, dinners, plays, sports—whatever you both like doing as a couple—will keep you closer together.
5. And yes, if you have the time, wrap your partner in a warm towel when he comes out of the shower.

Going out of your way to "sell" yourself and take care of your partner and relationship can reap sexual rewards. Remember, romance isn't just for Valentine's Day.

BE A HUMONGOUS FLIRT

A few months before I got married, a magazine advertisement caught my attention. It showed a very handsome couple in their fifties, smartly dressed and sitting on the patio of a French café. The wife was looking coquettishly at her husband, her fingers lovingly caressing his wrist. The headline for the ad read, "Flirt with your husband."

I honestly thought it was one of the coolest marriage notions I'd come across. At that moment, I made a fervent vow to flirt with my future husband for the rest of our married life. A year into our marriage, the ad was long forgotten; we had settled into our routine and flirting with my husband was a distant memory.

It's hard to dust off, pull out, and put into action your flirting mojo after the relationship gets comfortable. Perhaps you've never once flirted in your life (you probably have, you just didn't realize it). Nevertheless, flirting is an easy way to create happy, healthy, and sexy married-woman sex.

What Is Flirting?

I define flirting as the art of making someone else feel beautiful, and an exchange of positive energy between two people. Flirting allows both you and the receiver to feel positive about yourselves, and sexy. Flirting doesn't mean you give insincere compliments, or behave in any way that compromises your integrity. Rather, flirting is helping the other person feel special. *In your relationship, it's extremely important that you make a concerted effort to help your partner feel loved, appreciated, "beautiful," and special.* Flirting is a simple vehicle to keep up that positive exchange of energy.

Natural and unconscious flirts (not creepy flirts) are equal opportunists, flirting both with men and women. They smile, make eye contact, unabashedly laugh at jokes, and appropriately touch. They are exceedingly charming because they take a great interest in you, what you have to say, and what you are doing. You can't help but feel good with this lovely energy being directed at you.

Flirting with your partner doesn't have to mean batting your eyelashes, twirling your hair, or giggling incessantly at everything he says—he would probably panic and wonder who this imposter was.

As basic as it may sound, flirting with your partner is a way to make sure that you smile and make eye contact every day. Now be honest, when was the last time you laughed, smiled, and gazed lovingly into your partner's eyes? Instead of tuning him out when he discusses his favourite topic (the one that makes you want to hit your head against the wall out of boredom), this is the time to genuinely listen, ask prompting questions, and make comments. Have a bona fide conversation around a subject he finds fascinating.

Taking Innocent Flirting outside Your Relationship

Innocent flirting with someone other than your partner provides a wonderful feeling of self-esteem and energy, and a glow that can take sex from okay to WOW.

That said, flirting is a surprisingly sensitive topic for couples. You either think (to some extent) flirting is okay; or you think there should be zero flirting outside marriage. Before you skip this section, thinking this advice might be a little too liberal for you, please listen to why you should consider flirting outside your relationship.

One day while having coffee with a friend, I asked, "Why don't you and your husband try flirting?" A tiny look of terror crossed her face. She then uttered the words that many people admit when I broach the topic of flirting, "My husband wouldn't like it." Undaunted, I pressed the issue, "Why?"

She started squirming as if about to divulge deep dark bedroom secrets and replied, "He's just not that secure and, quite frankly, neither am I. I wouldn't like it if I saw another woman flirting with him." I walked away from the conversation musing on how her relationship and her sexuality could open vastly by the simple act of flirting.

Innocent flirting to me is like window shopping for those in a committed relationship. It fans the flames of romance and can successfully propel a healthy relationship forward over the long term.

Having a pro-flirting attitude creates great happy-couple energy.

Couples who began to flirt say they feel better about themselves, act sexier, and comment on how much more fun their partner is to be around. Their relationship is stronger and healthier as a result because they bring that positive energy home.

Jealousy

Jealousy, that green-eyed monster, stops most people from venturing into flirtation. Believe it or not, a *little* jealousy can make for great dynamic. It confirms there's affection in your relationship. Jealousy indicates there's excitement. That said, a well-balanced individual in a healthy relationship will not twist their jealousy into a full-blown disagreement.

What if you're the jealous type? Having strong feelings of jealousy is usually a sign that you don't have enough trust in your partner to be faithful to you. Lack of trust can stem from:

- Insecurity about your self-worth
- Not communicating the acceptable safe boundaries within your relationship
- Cheating on your partner (or others) in the past and projecting your behaviour onto your partner
- Your partner's history of cheating on you or other partners. (Please note: Even if they didn't have sex, creating an emotional attachment to another is in the cheating ballpark.)

Repairing and building trust so you are no longer jealous is possible. Check the Resources section on page 214 for books and websites.

Make a Flirting Agreement

A big part of successful flirting is having a mutual agreement about what is acceptable and unacceptable in your relationship. That means you must decide what flirting means to you, and communicate this to each other. Always remember, you two will go home together. All that positive, sexy energy you have created from flirting should take you into a fabulous, fun night *together*.

So how could your life and sex become that much better if you started to flirt? There's only one way to find out!

KEY POINTS

1. Being an equal in the bedroom means creating good intimacy habits outside the bedroom.
2. You need to make yourself a priority outside the bedroom before you can make yourself a priority inside the bedroom.
3. Frequent affectionate touch is essential to revitalizing your sex life and sex drive. When your partner is unexpectedly affectionate, watch your body's reaction. If you are freezing up, learn how to chill and lean into the touch.
4. During this transition time, look for the things he is doing right, instead of looking for what he is doing wrong.
5. Create a visual representation of what you want your sex life to be.
6. Romance means making kind gestures for your beloved. Do something kind for each other every day.
7. Flirting with your partner or someone else (as long as it's innocent) gives a wonderful feeling of self-esteem and energy, and a glow that can take sex from okay to WOW.

CHAPTER 7

Making Your Body
Your Sexual Ally

"Contrary to popular belief, most men don't get excited over zero per cent
body fat. Most men prefer women to be curvy and voluptuous."

—Brian Parker, Ph.D.

This chapter is about all the ways you've disengaged from your body.
Ironic really, as Mother Nature gave you all the tools—through your
body's unique sexual rhythm—to thoroughly enjoy sex over the long
term. It's time to start making your body your best sexual ally.

HOW TO LIKE YOUR STUFF IN THE BUFF

I've come to the conclusion that women don't have relationships with
their body. Rather, bodies are a catch-all for their scorn and are put
down every day.

Consider that 80 per cent of women are insecure about their body
image. Helping women to love their body is a tremendously tricky
topic. Women beg, "Yes, please, tell me fifty ways to look good naked."

"Yes, please, help me love my body so I can enjoy sex more" and then ignore my suggestions. Because when you look at your naked body in the mirror, your logical side gets tossed out the window and all of your fears, frustrations, and insecurities likely immobilize you. Let's take a closer look and try to sort through these body-hating issues together.

My Story—Intellect versus Emotion

Since I was a teenager I've had body hang-ups—I know, boo-hoo-hoo, get in line. Here's my cool intellect talking. I have a pear-shaped body complete with a tiny upper body, minuscule breasts, with rounded child-bearing hips and buttocks, shapely legs, and humongous feet. Because of some minor anorexic issues as a young woman (from which I recovered and learned), the control part of my brain has forced me to stay slim. Still, I've had cellulite on the backs of my legs since I was 13 years old. This means I've had over twenty-five years to get used to the fact that I have a pear-shaped body, teeny-tiny breasts, and cellulite on the backs of my legs.

Now, let's peek into my emotional side: When I'm having an insecure day and look in the mirror, my eyes immediately zoom in to my saddlebags. Heaven help if I masochistically turn around and see my orange-peel butt jiggling back at me. It doesn't matter that there are some really great aspects to my anatomy. I can focus (obsess would be a more appropriate word) only on the few things that are not "perfect."

Next comes the negative self-talk in my head. "What is the use when I look so fat and ugly? How could anyone possibly be sexy looking like this? Why don't I just go hide under a rock and never punish any other human being by having them look at this horrible excuse of a body?" Okay, okay, I'm not that bad.

Then I Got a Dose of Body Reality

In my last year of graduate school I took an advanced course in sex therapy. The class was to try an approach developed in the 1970s by the sex-therapist duo of William Hartman and Marilyn Fithian. With seven-foot-high mirrors at the front and back of the room, every individual in the class had to strip naked and describe from head to toe what they liked and disliked about their body.

Before that moment, while attending school, I had a lot of time to think about why women are so bothered about being naked in front of their partner. With fresh eyes, I read magazine articles with titles like "Ten Tricks to Hide Your Bulges"; watched Atkins and Weight Watchers commercials advocating losing weight before bikini season; and walked by cosmetics counters with miracle cures to eliminate unsightly cellulite. It became apparent that every woman every day is told numerous times just how unattractive her body is.

Also during that time, part of my schoolwork was to watch hundreds of hours of professionally shot California-artistic-style, free-love naked videos that starred average-looking people. I must admit it was difficult getting used to the unaugmented, "non-Hollywood" body types onscreen. Yet, for the first time ever, I saw just how beautiful the human body was before the advent of silicone implants, liposuction, and Botox injections. In fact, I noticed more beauty in the imperfections, as they made those people unique.

So there I was, taking off my clothes in front of my class. It was, to say the very least, absolutely nerve-wracking to strip while everyone watched. As tears streamed down my face and my whole body shook, I realized society's perfectionist values had a strong hold on me—it certainly didn't help that I was wearing my thong underwear, which only enhanced my orange-peel butt and thighs. I kept thinking how ludicrous my emotional outbreak was because I did exactly the same thing every day in the gym locker room.

Interestingly, none of the women in this class felt comfortable enough to get completely naked: We stripped down only to our bras and panties. And none of us could say a lot of things we liked about our bodies. It's quite scary and sad to think that we, future sex educators, mentors, and role models, could not speak about how we loved our vulvas.

The men, on the other hand, were pretty nonchalant about being naked and were happy to talk about their less-than-perfect figures as absolutely divine. And the relationship they had with their penis! Each guy had to praise his penis for at least a minute—I've never seen so much penis love. The difference in the men's and women's naked attitudes was a defining turning point.

In that moment, something in me snapped and my mind made a fundamental shift. For many days after the exercise, I was beyond angry, I was furious. Furious at all the wasted years of my life spent feeling inadequate about my body. Furious at how much I stifled my sexuality because I could not accept my imperfections as unique. Furious that I could not let people get close because my body insecurities pushed them away.

After the naked-perfectionist fury came the naked-reality calm. I would be lying if I said I always feel 100 per cent great about my body, because I don't. However, when I look in the mirror, I no longer hone in on my imperfections (much). Instead, I do my best to look at my body as beautiful, warts and all. By accepting my body, not surprisingly, I have an easier time letting my sensuality and sexuality come out and play.

What's Your Naked Paranoia Story?

Now that you've heard my story, what's yours? Unless you are among the 20 per cent of women who feel comfortable with her body, you undoubtedly can tell me why your belly flab, cellulite, wobbly thighs, or whatever you've deemed "wrong" about your body, is getting in the way of you enjoying sex.

I really wish that every woman could go through the same experience, get mad as heck, and say, "I'm not going to take this craziness anymore." As you are, understandably, not willingly to strip down naked in front of a bunch of people, what can you do to get real with what Mother Nature has so lovingly bestowed upon you? There are some suggestions below. But first . . .

Here's the "Love Your Body" Sermon

Why did feminists bother to burn their bras for you? The whole point of being equal in the bedroom is not to lie there like a stiff board and fulfill your wifely duty. Being able to partake in the sexual feast means allowing your body to absolutely abandon itself to sensual pleasures. It's silly to let a few body hang-ups hold you back from experiencing sex at its fullest.

A woman's body is as unique as her fingerprint—the yummy bits as well as the wobbly bits. So start facing your body issues and move into gorgeous sex.

It's Big Business To Keep You Feeling Insecure

Take a look around you at the thousands of companies whose multi-million-dollar advertising campaigns keep you teetering on the edge of insecurity. Weight-loss companies who show "average" women easily losing 60 pounds. Miracle eye wrinkle creams that keep your skin from looking old. Cellulite creams that take away unsightly orange-peel thighs. A woman can't turn around with out some company asking her if she's really sure that who she is really is good enough. The corporations have to because if the tables turned and over 80 per cent of women felt good about their bodies, they would go out of business.

Time to Look in the Mirror

As you're likely not going to strip down in front of a group, at least you can strip down in front of yourself. If you are truly serious about improving your body image, it's time to make a head-to-toe assessment—literally. The next time you have ten minutes alone, strip down naked in front of a full-length mirror. Starting from the top of your head with your hair and ending at your feet, list the things you like and dislike about your body, "I like my hair. I like my eyes. I like my ears. I don't like my nose."

If this seems like way too wacky an exercise and you want to skip this section, please stop for a minute and ask yourself why looking at yourself naked and listing what you deem to be "the good, the bad, and the ugly" seems so offputting. Once you have a list, here are some things to think about.

Eraser Myth: I believe women use their hated body part as an excuse to manifest some or all of their non-body-related insecurities. In workshops I ask women, "If you were able to take an eraser and wipe out the body part you don't like, and *poof*, like magic it became perfect, would you feel sexier?" The women immediately answer, "Well, yes of course." I look them straight in the eye and reply, "Are you sure about that? I think you would merely find a new body part to start hating."

Take the Zoom-In Test: Women tend to stand in front of the mirror and zoom in on all their wobbly bits—that is if they even have the energy to look at their "deformed body." Guess what? Reminding yourself 365 times a year that your body is ugly won't help you feel good about yourself.

Why Are You Being So Selfish? Instead, look at yourself through another's eyes. Your partner probably thinks you are gorgeous—why can't you?

Enthusiasm over Pudginess: I've talked to many women who hold back from trying new and exciting sexual positions for fear of looking chubby. Interestingly, men think an enthusiastic partner is a much bigger turn-on than one without the extra roll. Further, the chance of having an orgasm is drastically reduced if you're distracted by sucking in that tummy during sex.

Just Do It: If body image is an issue for you, just have sex. You'll be burning about 200 calories per hour while you're doing it.

The Last Body Frontier ... Your Vulva

Many years ago while teaching sex classes, I asked women to go home, look at their vulvas in a mirror, draw what they saw and then bring their drawing to the next class. I stopped assigning this exercise after only a few go-arounds. It wasn't because the women hated the exercise or that their look of fear was palatable (I can deal with that). I stopped because most women came to the next class without a drawing, most explaining they forgot or were too busy.

The profound aversion to having a relationship with her vulva is a big reason why so many women can't enjoy sex—remember above when the female doctoral students couldn't talk about their vulvas. What would it take for you to look at your vulva and then draw it? Ask yourself what's the difference between drawing your right hand and drawing your vulva—they're both body parts. Neither one should produce shame.

THE AWESOME THREE: SEXUAL DESIRE, SEXUAL AROUSAL, AND LIBIDO

I've lost count of how many women and men have said to me, "Since [fill in the blank—big event like having a baby, new job, marital disruption, prescription drugs, depression, the birth control pill] I've/my wife has lost my/her libido." In my head I'm thinking, of course you've lost your libido. Why in heaven's name were you counting on your libido in the first place?

Problem was, I took for granted these men and women knew the difference between a woman's sexual arousal, sexual desire, and libido. Pop culture tends to interchange these three terms as if they were the same thing. Is it any wonder people are confused? Therefore men/women/couples who profess to have lost their libido could be talking about losing their arousal, their desire, their libido, or all three.

First we'll look at your sexual libido, move on to sexual arousal, and then go to your sexual desire.

Sexual Libido
Your libido, what drives you to have sex and thus procreate, is made up of a complex array of hormones your body naturally produces. The average woman is born with about the same amount of estrogen, progesterone, testosterone, and a few other hormones (like oxytocin and

dopamine). Your hormones work harmoniously with one another with the monthly expectation that you're going to do your best to get pregnant. In the first year of a relationship, your libido is given a super-charged hormone boost (see page 21) that has you chomping at the bit for sex, making spur-of-the-moment sex so easy. It's Mother Nature's way of making you mate.

Two things work against your libido functioning at its maximum level after that initial year: You do not pay attention to your body's subtle signs, and the daily grind. As the rest of this chapter is dedicated to you paying more attention to how your body is trying to help you enjoy sex, for now we'll focus on the daily grind.

The hormones that make up your libido are so sensitive, walking out your door and experiencing normal day-to-day events almost guarantees that your libido will be negatively affected. Although men produce more testosterone, which gives their libidos an edge, they too are not immune to the negative effects of stress, etc. A major life change or some medications will upset the delicate hormonal balance. As you no longer have the I-must-have-sex-once-a-month-to-procreate to guide you, you come out the other side hardly ever having the urge to want sex.

However, pop culture perpetuates the idealistic romantic-love belief that if you truly loved your partner, your libido would take your sex through the good and bad times. Consequently, many couples sit on their duffs waiting for that magical sexy feeling to hit them—but it rarely does.

As much as Mother Nature wants recurring sex to be quick and easy, you cannot count on your libido to take you through the good and bad years. From this day forward, get the idea that sex should happen spontaneously out of your head and start paying more attention to your sexual arousal and sexual desire.

Sexual Arousal

Sexual arousal, or the physical side of sex, comprises all the signs your body shows to say it's ready for sex (see Appendix B). It's pretty darn easy to spot when a man is aroused, especially when he is wearing baggy pants. Where men's arousal is a simple matter of hydraulics, women's arousal is a matter of subtlety.

Generally as a woman gets into the sexual experience, her torso and other parts of her body will become flushed. Her breasts will become slightly engorged, as will her nipples, which will turn a deeper colour and become erect. The outer and inner lips of her vulva will swell, and if she's had a child the inner lips will turn a deeper, darker colour. Her vaginal canal will expand from its normal collapsed tube-like state, to form a tube and begin to sweat, which serves as lubrication. What you experience when you become aroused may include some of these signs as well as others.

Why Do Women Need Foreplay?

There's a logical explanation for why it takes women longer than men to get aroused. When a man becomes aroused, his penis, which is an approximately 6-inch tube, must swell up with blood. Although you would never say this to his face, the surface and space needed to engorge with blood is small and therefore doesn't take much time. For a healthy male to go from arousal to orgasm can take as little as two minutes. (I'm sure we've all experienced the bedsheet-gripping, hard-and-fast quickie. Yum!)

Women, on the other hand, have what is known as an orgasmic platform (the lower pelvic area), which engorges with blood. It's a much bigger surface area than his 6 inches and therefore takes a lot longer to become engorged and primed. How long? Generally if you're in a decent head space for sex where your brain isn't going a million miles an hour, it takes between ten to fifteen minutes of foreplay. Guess how long the average couple's sex lasts? Ten to fifteen minutes.

You might have had the experience where the sex is finished and you are left feeling aggravated, and wanting the sex to keep going. You're not alone. Your body was just winding itself up and then had no finish line to give it a release. It's confusing because if you experienced an orgasm at the start of the sex, you probably feel that was your release. Remember Shalina way back in Chapter 1? Just because you've had your single-woman-sex orgasm does not mean your body reached a state of arousal.

A big part of turning your sexual experience around is to understand what signs your body shows when it's becoming sexually aroused. Think of it as your body's arousal barometer. When sex is initiated you can look at your body signs and definitively say, "Yes, in fact, my body is into this sex" or, "I'm making a choice to have sex and skip my arousal" (which is crummy yet every couple has their sacrificial sex days).

The great news is that once your body does reach its optimum state of arousal, it's easier to achieve multiple orgasms (although physiologically some women don't have multiples; rather they experience one big orgasm). Because for as long as it takes for your orgasmic platform to engorge with blood, it takes just as long to become unengorged. By gently stimulating your inner lips, clitoris, and other sensitive arousal areas, if multiples are possible it's easy to knock off a few more orgasms.

Ask yourself the following:

1. Do you know what your body does and shows when it's in a state of arousal?
2. Are you making sure that you give yourself enough time to fully reach arousal?
3. When you think back to some of your best sex, can you remember how your body felt, acted, and reacted?

Sexual Desire (a.k.a. the "Wanna" Factor)

The number-one reason couples have sexual difficulty in North America is a lack of sexual desire, or a lack of "wanna," meaning there's a lot of anxiety before the sexual act about having sex, but once you start and get into it, it's not so bad.

Sexual desire, or the intellectual side of sex, is how you think about sex and all the thoughts you have about your sexual experience. It's the spark plug to get everything else working. What goes on in your head pretty much dictates the quality and quantity of your sex life. Perpetuating single-woman sex has the average busy woman dreading the sexual experience; hence she has little or no desire for the sexual act. Ironically lack of "wanna" prevents her from spending the time to get her body properly aroused. Can you see how this can turn into a vicious cycle?

While young men get pegged with only ever having sex on the brain (one fellow told me it was like white noise in his head) it might surprise you to know that men and women in their thirties think about sex about the same amount. However, there's a huge difference between how men think about sex and how women think about sex (surprise, surprise). When men think about sex (insert some bad 1970s porno music here) their thoughts are, generally, daydreams or fantasies. When women think about sex it's in terms of, "Shoot, has it been a week already?" terms. How women frame sex makes all the difference in our ability to enjoy the sexual experience. Couples struggling with opposite sex drives most likely experience problems because they have different levels of sexual desire.

Once you've been in a relationship for a while, and reached the single-woman-sex cycle of guilt/resentment sex, you hardly ever think about the sexual experience in positive terms. Foreplay becomes encased with dread, procrastination, and feeling used. It's not rocket science to say if sex is preceded by two hours of dread (or two weeks), guess what? There's no way you're going to enjoy or even be remotely interested in having sex.

So when you think about sex, what comes to mind first? Do you spend a lot of time procrastinating. Is your lack of "wanna" the problem? A big part of you creating the married-woman-sex experience is putting the "wanna" back into your head and thinking about sex in positive terms once again.

Recap

Libido, sexual arousal, and sexual desire all fundamentally affect your sexual experience. With the daily grind, you cannot count on your libido to get you sexually in the mood. Instead, you must understand how your body becomes aroused, how long it takes, and your body's cues. As well, you must look at how you think about sex; is it positive or negative?

GET TO KNOW YOUR BODY'S MONTHLY SEX CYCLE

Your body's menstrual cycle is an absolute wonder. Tapping into its hidden clues as to what you enjoy or don't enjoy sexually is simply a matter of paying attention.

A colleague of mine, Laura Wershler, is a zealous advocate of women shedding their birth control pill–popping ways and going *au naturel*. She believes the rhythm method of old—watching your body's cues and abstaining or using a condom when your body is ovulating—was too quickly given a bad rap and tossed out the window. She tirelessly campaigns for an updated version of the rhythm method, which leaves a woman's body chemicals free and does not affect with her natural menstrual cycle.

Women resist this birth control method because it seems like a lot of work to keep a menstrual journal, note changes in cervical discharge, pay attention to when the their ovary is releasing its monthly egg, as well as when their vaginal canal and cervix is more or less sensitive. Thing is, these signs are your body's natural sex cues. Unintentionally ignoring them probably has done a lot to damage Mother Nature's sexual rhythm and your enjoyment of sex.

Suppressing Pregnancy at the Cost of Sexuality

When I ask women do they know about how the birth control pill works, most give me a sheepish grin and say they aren't sure but, here's the kicker, their doctor says it's perfectly safe. Yes the pill is perfectly safe; yet for too many women, it causes them to lose interest in the sexual act.

Although you may in no way share Laura's belief system, have you ever sat back and wondered about how your menstrual cycle fundamentally affects your sexuality and sexual well-being? Or has your monthly visit from Aunt Flow been, "Shoot, that time of month. Have to go to the store to buy overpriced feminine protection. But at least I don't have to worry about having sex for the next five days or so"?

Let's take a look at how your hormones—estrogen, testosterone, progesterone, and oxytocin—work as a team to get your sexuality jacked up and good to go.

Estrogen: At the start of your 28-day menstrual cycle (the first day after your period has finished), your body begins producing estrogen, a hormone crucial to sexual development and a healthy reproductive system. It prepares your brain and body to be impregnated. So while ovulating, you've peaked in estrogen and consequently have a beautiful, juicy vagina that can take a whole lot of loving and still come back for more.

Testosterone: Testosterone promotes and stimulates sexual desire, hair growth, and energy level, but women produce it in much smaller quantities than men. The hormone rises during the second week (days 7 to 14) of your cycle to coincide with your peak ovulation. If you take a birth control pill it's likely that you'll have less testosterone available to you—one of the many reasons the pill decreases our libido.

Progesterone: Progesterone is produced in the ovaries and comes out in full force during the second half (days 14 to 28) of your menstrual cycle after you finish ovulating. It stimulates the thickening of the uterine lining in anticipation of a possible pregnancy. If you do become pregnant, progesterone helps the fertilized egg implant in the uterus. If you don't become pregnant, progesterone curbs your sexual desire and acts to partially reverse the effects of testosterone in your system. Your body and vagina become more sensitive and hard-thrusting sex might be uncomfortable.

Oxytocin: Women's nurture and connection hormone, oxytocin is produced when you go into labour. The hormone helps you bond with your baby and stimulates milk production for breast-feeding. Intimacy releases oxytocin, which is the main reason women want and need to have a connection moment (foreplay/ intimacy) to connect before they can have sex. Both men and women release oxytocin when orgasming, helping them to feel closer after the sexual act.

How you want to be touched, treated, and needed (for example, soft or strong stroking or penile thrusting) coincides with your body's changing hormone levels. Although this is unrelated to your sexual rhythm (which I will explain shortly), not understanding how your menstrual cycle works will most certainly affect how much and how often you want sex.

How It All Comes Together

Generally, the libido works this way: After a woman finishes her period, her estrogen begins ramping up. Estrogen creates the best environment to have sex: it softens the cervix, and allows for your best lubrication. Essentially, estrogen is preparing your orgasmic platform to be in top shape.

Fourteen days after your period (unless you have something different than a 28-day menstrual cycle), comes your ovulation during which an egg (ova) starts to travel down one of your fallopian tubes. Your estrogen and testosterone have peaked, so your libido ensures that everything points to you having your "horny day." Oh come on, admit it, there's at least one day of the month that you have a stronger urge to jump anything that moves. At that point, having raunchy, deep-thrusting sex is A-okay in your books because your vagina is a baby-making love machine.

After ovulation, you release progesterone, which either helps the egg stick to the uterine wall or shuts down breeding operations until next month. Progesterone slowly turns your vagina less and less juicy from where it was only a few days ago. When you are close to your period and progesterone has peaked, your body, breasts, and vagina are more sensitive, so tender lovemaking is the name of the game.

Some women report their horny day as just before their period. Other women report feeling randy as soon as their period has finished. Figure out when you feel at your sexual prime. Tuning into your body's natural cycle means you have more control over the type of sex you're having. So you can say to your partner when your vagina isn't so juicy, "I know only a few days ago I couldn't get enough of the wild thrusting, but now I need it to be more gentle."

Your Hormones as You Age

In Your Teens: Your body had just started to menstruate and you (and everyone you lived with) were getting used to the monthly hormonal fluctuations. You were temperamental, super horny, and super emotional. Between facial pimples, crazy PMS symptoms, mood swings (oh gosh, the mood swings), and cramps, was it any wonder you were a walking drama queen?

In Your Twenties: One of the reasons women long for their twenties again is that their hormones are at their best. Your menstrual cycle ran like clockwork with your estrogen and progesterone production behaving themselves. Your body's response to hormones was less dramatic and you'd had a few years to get used to your 28-day cycle.

In Your Thirties: You become more alert to your PMS symptoms. Many women today are putting off having children until their thirties. Because a shift in societal values, this is when the biological clock starts to tick very loudly. If you do decide to have children, hormones go berserk for the entire pregnancy, plus up to a year after the baby is born—especially if you decide to breast-feed. That's almost two years of unpredictable hormones multiplied by however many children you choose to have. In your mid- to late thirties you may have more testosterone available, which can ramp up your libido.

In Your Forties: **When you reach your mid-forties, you may start peri-menopause.** Perimenopause starts preparing your reproductive system to shut down and move into menopause. Typically it starts four to five years before menopause, ten years being the extreme. The problem? Your estrogen and progesterone levels begin to fluctuate erratically. Suddenly you are dealing with the same symptoms as menopause—irregular periods, hot flashes, and night sweats—but on an inconsistent basis. If that isn't enough, one minute you have a nice juicy vagina and the next it's dried-up and sensitive. One minute you're totally into the sex, the next it hurts. Trying to keep up is confusing and frustrating for both you and your partner—this is where strong communication is key.

One of the benefits to this time is you produce less oxytocin. Meaning you no longer have an innate need to nurture everyone but yourself. You start looking at what you want out of life and don't feel as selfish.

When You're Fifty and Older: **Once you've reached menopause—going at least a year without your menstrual period—you will have to learn to deal with your changed body's connection to sex. Every woman's journey through menopause is unique and it would be fool-hardy to give an umbrella suggestion on body mechanics. The Resource section has a list of reference books if you want more information.

Simple Questions to Start Becoming Menstrual Literate

1. Is yours a 28-day cycle?
2. Can you pinpoint the day your last period began?
3. Can you tell the viscosity of your vagina's discharge in relation to where you are in your period?
4. Can you feel when your monthly egg is breaking free of the ovary?
5. For how many days do your breasts feel tender before you start your period?

6. Do you recognize and acknowlege the days when you want to be touched softer or harder or not at all?

Your menstrual period plays such an important role in your enjoyment of sex. By paying attention to your body's natural hormonal rhythm, you can start creating the best-quality sex.

YOUR BODY'S SEXUAL RHYTHM

Depending on your stage of life, having sex once a week may be an unrealistic expectation. The number of times you engage in intercourse per day, week, month, or year won't be constant throughout your life but, rather, something that works with your current life situation. During times of major change or upheaval, maintaining an intimate connection that has little or nothing to do with intercourse is perfectly acceptable. I'll give you a moment to let that sink in.

(And no, this is NOT the time to put the book down, run to your spouse, and say, "I told you so." Although, I agree, it would feel nice to rub it in.)

Chances are, you never thought about your unique sexual rhythm, hoping your libido would carry you through. It's time to become in tune with your body and come to terms with when and how much you want sex.

What Is a Sexual Rhythm?

Sexual rhythm is a mind, body, spirit check-in to understand how much sex can be accommodated with your current life situation. Although sexual intercourse is important for your well-being as a couple, frequency is not necessarily the greatest common value. Rather, you aspire for maintaining a constant emotional and intimate connection.

Said more simply: Depending on your life's circumstance, frequent intercourse may not be possible; regardless, you must maintain an intimate connection.

When you have little to no responsibility, your sexual rhythm can see you having sex often and for hours at a time. Major changes or upheavals, like babies, promotions, or moving, mean sex will be irregular and an uphill battle to maintain any sort of regularity. When you aren't experiencing major changes and are gliding along without too many worries, sex on a weekly or at least on a regular basis is easily doable.

Whose Sexual Rhythm—Yours or His?

Most women pay attention only to their partner's sexual rhythm—how much sex he wants, needs, or desires. It's true that it's important to accommodate his needs; however, he is probably the only person in your relationship stating his needs. The squeaky wheel always gets the grease. Not paying attention to what your mind, body, and soul need from sex sets you up for a negative single-woman-sex experience.

Reactive versus Proactive Sex

If you've been coasting along or painstakingly making sure to have sex once per week, it has likely created a negative reaction toward sex. When you understand your sexual rhythm, it puts you in the driver's seat, where you anticipate your current stage of life and make the necessary adjustments. Here are two scenarios.

Reactive: When a major upheaval happens (child, promotion, illness, etc.) you're scrambling just to keep your sanity and life together. You know it's important to have sex with your partner but right now you feel so overwhelmed that sex is a nuisance. You have sex not because you want to but rather to avoid feeling bad.

Proactive: You sit down with your partner and constructively communicate (Chapter 5) what your sex will be (e.g., for the next six months to a year sex will be erratic). You figure out how you'll keep an intimate connection with each other. Then together, make a date on your calendar to come together and figure out a new strategy in six months.

When you know sex will happen within the frequency that feels good for you, you've discussed and negotiated with your partner, you go into sex upbeat, positive, wanting to participate, and enjoy because the underlying pressure and guilt to have sex is gone. When the upheaval period is over, because you've set a date in your calendar to come back and discuss your new life status, you can happily acknowledge it's time to start having sex on a more regular basis.

The Trouble with Being Reactive

When you experience a major life upheaval, you never discuss (except during a disagreement) why sex has dropped off the radar. Because you're simply coasting along, poor communication, poor emotional patterns, and poor sex become the norm.

Then when the upheaval ends and you're finally sailing smooth water, it takes forever to reconnect and make sex a habit again—if that's even possible. Suddenly, life throws you yet another upheaval and you're back at square one. This is why people say, "since the kids," "since the illness," "since [fill in the blank], we don't have sex any-more." It's not the major life upheaval but being reactive that has done the damage.

Proactive Means You Can No Longer Sit On Your Butt and Be a Victim

Being proactive is one of those "stitch in time saves you nine" ideals. Doing a little work up front reaps great rewards. But you have to proac-tively stay on top or at least be aware of your current sexual rhythm and be in constant communication with your partner.

Sex Is a Team Sport

When I speak to women about their sexual rhythms, inevitably one (or more) pipes up and cries, "My husband's not going to like if I want sex once a month and he wants sex twice a week." Of course he's not going to be happy. You've set an expectation, up to this point, that you both rely on his sexual rhythm.

Married-woman sex means your sexual needs are equal to his. You're half of the sexual experience. Taking into account your sexual rhythms means you're changing the sex-frequency rules.

Even though it comes down to your wants versus his wants, it doesn't have to be a struggle. First the passive-aggressive avoiding-sex scenario will be eliminated from your relationship, because you are proactively working together. Second, paying attention to your needs can change your whole perspective of the sexual experience. When you have an equal say in the quality and quantity of your sex, you come to anticipate that sex instead of dreading it.

Also, occasionally your sexual rhythm might have you wanting sex three or more times a week. If you're being only reactive, those I-can't-get-enough-sex times are never allowed to surface.

Here's How to Start

It's time you understand what your body is saying to you about having sex at this point in your life. Once you get into the groove, it's not complicated. Here's how:

1. Do a sexual-rhythm body check-in every six months. Take a look at your current life situation. Is it: hectic, coasting, or not much going on?
2. You're probably thinking there's no way you can remember to check in with your body every six months. If it helps, mark it in your calendar.
3. After you start paying attention to what your body, mind, and soul want from sex and intimacy, communicate this to your partner.
4. Keep up the positive, loving outside-the-bedroom connection.

It's funny how the things that are the least sexy make for the best sex. Getting into the habit of having an ongoing dialogue with your partner about your sexual feelings and his sexual feelings is one of the best boosts you can give to your relationship. It can be as simple as, "How are you feeling about sex today?" Or "After that long stretch of sporadic sex, I'm ready to get back on that horse and have some crazy sex. Let's rent a hotel room for the night to put sex into high gear."

Even if you are not having sex once a week, you need to keep the intimate connection with your partner alive and strong. That way both of you can segue in and out of both of your sexual rhythms without too much relationship upheaval.

REAWAKENING THE BIG FIVE BODY SENSES

Have you numbed your five senses? Chances are you have, and it's making a big difference in your ability to enjoy sex. Busy women tend to live inside our heads, leaving our bodies to dangle as if they were invisible. I believe the technical term is a "floating head."

Multi-Tasking is Your Bedroom Nemesis

If you're a busy woman then you are no doubt a fabulous multi-tasker, effortlessly able to juggle ten things—with a justified sense of pride. It's some of the only praise we'll allow ourselves to accept and believe. Naturally, we feel we're helping ourselves and everyone else around us with this wonderful ability. And many times we are, except when it comes to bedroom exploits.

When it comes time for sex it can be extremely difficult to calm your brain. Consequently, it takes you longer to become aroused and, before you know it, the sex act is over and your body ends up with a big fat goose-egg worth of pleasure.

My Sister's Story

At one point my younger sister had three children under the age of five (ack!). It was impressive to watch her keep it all together: She was a wonderful mom, good wife, and a super-star employee, and complained very little. I wanted to give her a treat and remembered that in her single days she hogged the bathroom, taking two- or three-hour baths. For Mother's Day I went out and bought her a fancy bath basket, complete with a selection of lotions and potions. Attached was a note: "Make sure to spoil yourself and take a half-hour bath once a week."

A few weeks later I phoned and asked, "How did you like your bath basket?" Sheepishly she mumbled that she hadn't quite gotten to it yet. A few months later I asked again, "Hey, how did you like your bath basket?" Very embarrassed, she confessed, "Well ... actually ... I'm saving it for a special occasion." A special occasion? What the heck does that mean? A confused and hurt "Oh" was all I could come back with.

When I get to this point in the story during seminars, I immediately know the mothers in the audience—they're the ones rolling their eyes, thinking how silly it was for me to suppose my busy sister could possibly take time out for a once-a-week (or even once-a-year) bath.

Yes, when I gave the basket of goodies I didn't have children and had no clue about the level of responsibility. Nevertheless, although my sister was giving and gives 110 per cent to make a wonderful life for her family, she didn't feel justified to indulge herself in something she really enjoyed for thirty minutes every week. I hope you can concede there's something wacky about that logic.

What's worse is while in these time-starved periods of life, women create bad habits and usually never get back into making herself a priority. Instead my sister resigned herself to the belief that it's a woman's plight to place herself second.

Months later, my sister and I talked about this. We both agreed this is a complicated issue with no easy answer. Intellectually my sister understands this societal construct is complete and utter baloney. Emotionally though—and I sometimes wonder if there's a bit of hardwiring thrown in to boot—it made my sister worry that she would come off as narcissistic or overly self-indulgent.

She told me that even though she wanted to spend more time on herself, at this point it wasn't possible. However, as a concession to start taking care of herself (because I wouldn't get off her back), she started dabbing a bit of aromatic cuticle cream on just before bed. It took only a few seconds and the wonderful fragrance gave her a small boost before bedtime.

Your Body Needs Your Help

Now let's get back to this idea of a floating head. Alongside being forced into multi-tasking martyrdom, it's frowned upon that we even indulge a tiny bit. This is a recipe for disaster when it comes to your bedtime pleasures: Changing from floating head to sex goddess in sixty seconds or less just ain't going to happen.

"Being Present" Break

You need to start playing nice with your body, giving it some much-needed TLC to decompress. It doesn't have to take a lot of time, effort, or money. You can spend as little as ten seconds every day bringing out one of your five senses: touch, taste, smell, hearing, and seeing (see page 125 for some great ideas).

Make an effort to have daily ten-second "being present" breaks. You can fit this in while doing your normal routine. Start tasting the food you eat, being aware while in the shower to feel the soap running down your body, feeling the hard keyboard under your fingertips as you type. Allow your senses to feel, well, sensual.

Do your best to focus on your body's sensations. What feels good to your touch? Which favourite food makes your taste buds dance? The merits of aromatherapy have been known for centuries, so what smell relaxes your body instantly? What music or sound calms you down or revs you up? What enlivens your visual senses? Most importantly, do you *allow* yourself to feel this wonderfulness? If not, seriously consider why you are denying yourself this simple pleasure of sensuality.

In her book *Fearless Sex,* Joy Davidson writes, "Sensory self-soothing should be done mindfully; that is, with full attention given to each act. If you're petting your dog, feel the soft texture of his coat, the rise and fall of his chest as he inhales and exhales. If you're baking bread, immerse yourself in each detail. . . . You want to train yourself to move beyond the habit of doing one thing while with your body while your mind remains hopelessly fixated on the object of your obsession."

For goodness' sakes, don't be like my sister and save your indulgences for special occasions. Make sure to take a little time every day to be present in your body. When you get used to feeling your body and the sensations it provides, getting out of your brain and allowing your body to become aroused when sex is initiated will become easier.

From this point forward, how will you make your body your sexual ally? Even though you have a thousand things to worry about every second of the day, there comes a point when you must stop being a floating head. Getting back into the rhythms of your body simply means paying attention.

KEY POINTS

1. Have you let your body's so-called imperfections get in the way of enjoying sex as much as possible?
2. As you probably can't count on your libido to see your sex life through the long term, how will you start paying attention to your sexual arousal and sexual desire?
3. Throughout your menstrual cycle, how you want to be touched (i.e., gently or powerfully) coincides with your body's changing hormone levels.
4. How much you want sex is in direct correlation to what is going on in your life. As your sexual rhythm changes constantly, you need to factor in your body's wants, needs, and desires for sex.
5. Women tend to numb themselves from the neck down, becoming floating heads. It's important for you to make sure to consciously experience at least one of your five senses each and every day.

CHAPTER 8

Having Sex on Your Terms

"If I could do it over again, I would have brought humour and laughter into our relationship much sooner."

— Jude Bown, married twenty years

Although your partner's wants and needs are important, **sex has to** also be on your terms. It's time to make sex work around you. Instead of playing a passive role, you need to step up to the plate and become an active player in how your sex unfolds weekly, monthly, and throughout the years.

Build Your Sexual Momentum

Most couples are anxious to know how often the average couple has sex. Unfortunately, there are too many variables to give an absolute number. But at least once a year the headlines announce, "The Acme Condom sex survey found the average North American couple has sex at least two to three times per week." I wonder who these "average" people are. It may be true of my friends with a hearty sex life, but it isn't for any typical couple I know. Indeed in my experience the average couple struggles to have sex once every couple of weeks. These pop-culture studies lack scientific credibility.

So when I tell people there is no average number for how often couples have sex, they are disheartened. They're desperate for a bench-mark to see how "normal" their own relationship is. If they're having more than "average," they feel like heroes. If they're having less sex than "average," the accusations and fights begin.

Rating your sex life against nameless couples, who most likely lied on the survey to save face, is crazy. Really, if some stranger asked you point-blank how often you had sex, you either wouldn't tell her or you'd lie.

Measuring your sexual success against "everyone else" is a no-win situation, and a surefire way to create a lot of negative feelings. Yet couples have no other barometer by which to measure what is sexually normal. They don't trust in themselves or their relationship to tell the truth that works for them at this time in their lives.

What's in a Number?

I'm against having sex "X" times per week, month, or year as a meas-urement of your sexual success. Too often numbers make women feel forced into having quota-filling sex, and if they aren't keeping up, they have one more thing to feel guilty about. Numbers mean the partner who wants sex more often can hold the lack of times they had sex over the other partner.

I believe numbers are a guy thing; generally men need to measure their sexual success in concrete terms. By and large, women measure sexual success by the feelings and interactions during and between the sexual encounters.

A woman in one of my courses confided, "My husband just came through prostate cancer. Now he wants sex all the time because he says it's beneficial for his prostate. I don't want to be forced to have sex two to three times per week just to appease his bloody prostate." Yes, overcoming cancer is a major event that needs to be celebrated. Celebrating is much easier when it isn't used, unintentionally, to get guilt sex. He's thinking numbers and she's feeling negative feelings between each sexual encounter. She's not having sex on her terms; she's having sex on his prostate's terms.

MAKING SEX A HABIT: A WOMAN'S LITTLE-KNOWN SECRET

Although I am against numbers, it's imperative that busy couples make sex a habit by shifting their sexual-habit sensibility. Having sex on your terms means you create a habit of having sex because you desire sex—not because you have to meet a number. Let me explain.

It's important to understand the differences between men and women around their need to orgasm. Men are biologically predisposed to orgasm/ejaculate every twenty-four to forty-eight hours to spread their seed and create as many offspring as possible. Women are much more selective about whom they mate with.

Women are hard-wired in a way that the longer we go without an orgasm, the less we need one. (Are some things in your sexual life making a little more sense now?) Equally, the more a woman orgasms, the more she will want to have an orgasm. *You, unlike your guy, must build an orgasm momentum.*

Perhaps you've been in a situation where sex has been erratic over the last few months and settled for "just get it over with so I can go to sleep" sex. Suddenly, one day, you're in a horny state of mind and you end up having a great experience, with a mind-blowing orgasm to boot. These are the times when you will inevitably think, "Why aren't we having sex more often? That was bloody brilliant. I feel so connected to my partner. We need to do that again but soon!"

Make Sex a Habit for You, Not Necessarily for Him

Making sex a habit is for you and your pleasure, not necessarily his. Being selfish in bed, taking what you want, and letting your partner be damned is something we learned that good girls don't do. Instead, good girls have sex because it will benefit their partner's prostate, not because it's their right to make the sex about their satisfaction.

In her book *Fearless Sex*, Joy Davidson boldly explains, "In a female-centred world, having sex would mean having your breasts stroked, your thighs caressed, your clit licked, your G-spot stimulated, your feet massaged. A penis might or might not be involved. It would mean kissing until you feel faint. It would mean orgasms of the soul and spirit as well as the body. It would mean mind-blowing, heart-stopping, ecstatic sensation with no pressure to orgasm at all."

Making sex a habit for your sexual momentum means you are a more willing, able, and participatory partner. If you're concerned about your partner's feelings, don't be. I would bet my house your partner will be completely and utterly into your selfishness. Your selfishness means you want sex. He couldn't ask for much more than that.

PUT YOUR BACK INTO IT

Thinking about getting your sex life on track is relatively easy; the actual doing is another matter. I have no doubt that you can make this happen. However, the major obstacle stopping you from taking the jump will be you. When your body and mind start their usual rebelling against having sex, it's time to ramp up your sex energy.

You see, while your intellect will always catch on quickly, your body is slower. Single-woman sex is like an old familiar friend you've outgrown; you don't necessarily want that person in your life anymore but there is a level of comfort that you can't seem to shake.

Be Prepared for Failure
It's taken years for you to build up these feelings about sex in general, as well as sex with your partner. It will not, I repeat *not*, change overnight even though you are making a concerted effort.

This is probably one of the more discouraging parts of this process.

You have all these great intentions, want to have super sex, are doing your best to make it happen, and, realistically, the first few times you have sex it might not be so great—or it might be fantabulous!

The "Wanna" Lag Time

Your desire, or the "wanna" part of sex, can have a long lag time. Logically, you've made some choices on creating a better sex life. As excited as you may be, one tiny little incident that had you fighting mad and avoiding sex in the first place will snap you right back to where you were.

When your body goes into its "I'm not going to enjoy sex" routine, you must put your back into it, so to speak, and not give in to your body's negative pressure. It is critical to reject the idea that all this nonsense isn't working. Remember your ultimate goal: to have married-woman sex.

Re-create Your Brain's Hard-wiring

Did you know that it takes at least twenty-eight days to form a new habit and that's only if you're doing it every day? The more you do something, the more cells the brain assigns to that task. It's at this point you're deciding where you want to assign your brain cells: to loving sex or to not. Be warned: All those negative emotions that you have been dealing with are still around, so you'll have to really concentrate on your goal and continue building good habits.

Fake It Till You Make It

At first you might even have to fake it till you make it. (Never under any circumstance have sex when you don't want to. Having guilt, resentment, or quota-filling sex is what most likely got you into this mess in the first place.) When moving your sex forward, you're facing a big bump in the road. As long as the sex is on your terms, then the only thing for you to do is to rev your engine and drive. You've probably heard that when you're having a bad day you should slap a smile on your face. With that one act, your entire physiology changes and your mood lightens. Sexual desire works on the same principle: mind over body. The more you don't feel like having sex, the more you must encourage yourself to fully and actively participate. The more effort you put into it, the likelier you will start to enjoy it.

Toss Your Superwoman Pride

Having sex on your terms may mean leaving perfectionist tendencies at the door. Perhaps you and I should take a lesson from the 1980s women who went out to stake a claim in the professional world. They straddled the line between living up to June Cleaver's version of perfect motherhood and thumbing their noses at society, boldly exclaiming, "I'll show the world I can be a career gal." One lady I know simultaneously brought up three small children, worked on her Ph.D. thesis, and held down three jobs.

Not surprisingly, the 1980s woman's new agenda came at the cost of her sexuality. With only twenty-four hours in a day, full-time work and full-time motherhood usually meant zero time for pleasure. Then for at least the next ten years the media extol the virtues of living and leading a balanced lifestyle—giving the average busy woman something else to feel guilty about. Thank goodness balance experts are finally admitting that it's very difficult to live your life in complete balance.

In their book *Sexy Mamas*, Cathy Winks and Anne Semans write, "Supermom is a complete nightmare of a role model, and we say— wake up! The pressure to live up to the ideal is killing us.... We invite you NOT to be Supermom. Let something go. Do for yourself. Be selfish. So what if you can't leap tall buildings in a single bound? You will love yourself, and from there all good things will come."

Women who decide they can't be everything to everyone enjoy having sex with their partners again. They realize that pushing themselves to the brink over and over again leaves no desire for sexual intimacy.

When you're caught up in your everyday multi-tasking frenzy, your brain may take your body hostage and not allow you to enjoy sex. That's one of reasons sex experts beg you to slow down before sex and incorporate foreplay. You need to engage your body, to be fully present and consequently fully aroused to the sexual experience so it will be as enjoyable for you as your partner.

Why Women Don't Have an On-Off Switch

You've probably figured out switching your brain from 1,001 things to sex is difficult. In her book *The Female Brain,* Dr. Louann Brizendine explains that "Female sexual turn-on begins, ironically, with a brain turn-off. The impulses can rush to the pleasure centers and trigger an orgasm only if the amygdale—the fear and anxiety center of the brain—has been deactivated. Before the amygdale has been turned off, any last-minute worry—about work, kids, about schedules, about getting dinner on the table—can interrupt the march toward orgasm."

Create Sex Triggers

Just like every other impulse sent to the brain to tell it what's going on with your body, you need to send a signal to your brain that it's time for sex. The more times you use the same sequence of events, the easier it'll be for your brain to rewire itself into the new habit.

Do you remember as a kid what you were told to do if you were ever on fire? Stop, drop, and roll. When it's time to have sex and your brain is in hyper-warp, think of it as a fire drill: stop, breathe, refocus. Okay, it doesn't trip off your tongue, but I hope it will be more fun.

Stop

Before the big moment, create a ritual to get out of your head and wake up your five senses: touch, hearing, sight, taste, and smell. Your ritual could include lighting a scented candle, putting on some music, taking a sudsy shower, or eating chocolate (mmm, chocolate). Each serves as a mental trigger for you to understand it's time to calm down.

If the sex is spontaneous and you don't have time for the ritual, you need to say out loud, "Stop," which may feel silly; however, saying it silently just doesn't have the same impact. Saying it aloud will literally jerk your brain to attention and better ease you into being present.

Breathe

Taking good deep breaths is your fastest, easiest way to calm your brain and your body. Stressed people tend to breathe from their diaphragm and take shallow breaths, giving themselves minimal oxygen. Discreetly taking ten deep breaths, in through the nose and out through the mouth, will have you quite relaxed in less than a minute. You can't get any more instant gratification than that.

Refocus

After this preparation, the first time you use the stop, breathe, refocus technique, your mind will probably start the old and familiar racing. If you can't calm yourself again, discreetly pinch (yes pinch) your forearm—the shock that will snap you into the present. Then encourage your partner to stroke your body: your hips, buttocks, the small of your back. Do not rush toward sex. Train yourself to relax (or chill) and lean into the good feelings. Do your best to get over the hump of, "Let's just get this over with."

SEVEN-DAY SEX CHALLENGE

If you're one of those people who want a really easy way to get sex back on track, here it is. Commit to having sex with your partner at least once per day for the next seven days in a row. Yeah, you read that right. Have sex every day for the next seven days. You'll be amazed and surprised by the results.

Laura Corn suggests this in her book *The Great American Sex Diet*. She also describes how she and her partner reached a two-month, no-sex dry patch. She decided to give him sympathy sex because she felt so bad. Much to her surprise, she enjoyed it. On the spot she decided to have sex with him every day for the next seven days. Gleefully Corn describes the results, "Well, I just felt better and better with every passing day, energized in my body, relaxed in my mind, and completely in touch with myself at the core of my spirit. What was happening? Was this the power of sex?"

Since reading her book, I've given this advice to many couples. Admittedly, some walk away shaking their heads. However, the couples who've taken this advice and run with it, without exception, report back with the same results as Corn. As a couple they feel closer, more energized, happier, and willing to take on any sex challenge facing them.

If you're thinking it sounds nice in theory but you could never make this work in your relationship, ask yourself: What do I have to lose? Maybe more importantly: What do I have to gain? Having sex seven days in a row—especially if it's your decision—can bring about only good feelings. Instead of actively avoiding and creating procrastination sex, you're actively looking for ways to make it happen. It's propelling you to make a complete shift in your current sexual sensibility. Remember, it's not the sex but your feelings toward the sex that you want to turn around.

Sex Becomes a Team Sport

This is a great idea because it turns sex from a me-versus-you dynamic into a team sport, like the early days of your relationship.

- You are working as a couple toward a common purpose—instead of against each other.
- Sex is no longer a power struggle and you call a temporary truce because both of you agree to have sex for seven days.
- Both of you have to put in effort and by doing so you both agree to initiate and make sex fun.
- Seven days of sex means you're in a constant state of desire—your body, mind, and spirit are already in the sex groove. It's a good ego boost to know you still can desire sex and it gives you the courage to try other ideas in this book.

Seven Days of Communication

As we've already discussed, great sex starts with great communication. Here's a fun way to get both your sex and communication about sex started. Part of the fun is charting your sex course. You are both committed to having sex for the next seven days, so together you must plan your course of action. Put any and all expectations on the table. This is such a fabulous way to take a baby step in your sexual communication.

Discuss and try the following:

- Take turns surprising one another.
- Have a mutual agreement to lock the door to your bedroom and get busy.
- Mix it up with some morning sex, afternoon sex, and evening sex.
- Make sure to incorporate massages, baths, and picnics as part of foreplay
- Whether to bring in accoutrements like sex toys or board games.

By doing the seven-day sex challenge, you'll be using everything you've learned from this book. It will also set an extremely healthy precedent to work through the rest of the book. By having sex seven days in a row, your sexual relationship will re-ignite.

How Do You Kick-Start Sex in a Non-Starter?

We've talked about why it's so important for you to get the momentum going in your sex life—for your sexual satisfaction rather than his. Seven days of sex is the fast, easy way to put your propeller in the water. Yet, what if you or your partner is not interested in that option? Or after the seven days of amazing sex, you're back at square one, not knowing how to initiate sex. This is where you have to look at your couple patterns of initiation and whether initiating sex stops you dead in your tracks.

There's nothing more awkward than trying to initiate in a lacklustre sex life. Figuring out where to and how to get the ball rolling in your sex life is indeed a daunting task.

Although you both want the same thing, and you're looking at each other and thinking it, you feel immobilized and can't move forward.

Who Initiates Sex

Who initiates sex in your relationship? Couples surveyed said, ideally, they'd like both partners to initiate equally. Yet, as we already discussed, people tend to attract their personality opposite. As a result, one person will be more assertive and tend to do the bulk of bedroom initiation. Unwittingly, couples settle in an Initiator-Pursued bonding pattern. One person always initiating sex becomes dull quickly.

In their book *Sex Matters for Women*, Sallie Foley, Sally Kope, and Dennis Sugrue write, "But because sex is such a loaded issue in our society, many people find it awkward to initiate lovemaking, even when they desire it and thoroughly enjoy it.... The burden of feeling awkward or ashamed of wanting it too much inhibits them. If a woman or man feels sexually insecure, initiating sex can be intimidating. The ever-present possibility of being turned down or ridiculed makes the overture too scary."

The Initiator begins to question, "Does this person even find me attractive?" This cycle becomes even more destructive when the Initiator has had enough and starts to nag the Pursued. Both feel hopeless and helpless; the Pursued shuts down, digging in her heels. The result is a toxic power struggle, with both people dredging up hurt feelings and putting up walls. Sex comes to a screeching halt with neither person knowing how to climb out of the non-initiating hole.

Being an Equal-Opportunity Initiator

Having sex on your terms means you need to say when you want to have sex. Therefore it's important that you make a conscious effort to proactively start initiating sex. Becoming an equal-opportunity Initiator may be uncomfortable at first. Where do you start?

Get the Facts

Start with the facts. Figure out how many times a month you initiate (remember it's about increasing your sexual momentum). Make a commitment to raise that number over the next six months. If you initiate once every couple of months, resolve to initiate once a month.

Remember that with goals, having a specific number helps steel your resolve.

Set Your Boundaries

Next, set your boundaries. If your partner overtly or covertly bugs you about not initiating—sarcastic jabs, sighs, slamming of doors—wait until he calms down and tell him to stop, and that you're doing your best to create a new dynamic. Explain that a big part of the problem is his constant negative reinforcement, which is most likely paralyzing your ability to initiate. If he doesn't believe you, ask him to read this section of the book.

Take Baby Steps

Now it's time to take action. Start small to build up your confidence. Give him a lingering kiss when he doesn't expect it. When he's doing a chore, go and wrap your arms around him and give him a suggestive squeeze. These baby steps are not about having sex; they are a way for you to get comfortable and set up a dynamic of fun and play between the two of you.

Your Partner's Reaction

There are two ways your partner can react to the new and improved initiating you. The first, and best, way is that he'll be overjoyed. The second, and more human, way is for him to play it cool and passive-aggressive: "You've punished me for so long, now you are going to get a taste of your own medicine." Don't panic, internalize, or get into new destructive habits if you get an unenthusiastic response. This is simply the awkward part of transforming new habits.

It's Time to Strut Your Stuff

Once you become more confident with the baby steps, it's time to strut your stuff. This confident initiating demands some planning on your part. Set a night aside and, beforehand, decide what you'd like to happen. Planning gives you an opportunity to think about how you're going to initiate. What are you going to say? What are you going to do? How are you going to do it?

Think of as your time to start positively anticipating sex. Anticipation means piquing your lover's curiosity by dropping sex clues during the day, keeping him guessing, and giving him something to look forward to. That's not so bad.

Be Specific, Clear, and Positive

Dr. Patricia Love and Jo Robinson, co-authors of *Hot Monogamy*, give this tip: "Be more direct in asking for sex ... You might say to your partner, 'I'm feeling really sexy tonight. I'd like to make love to you,' or 'I would really appreciate it if we had sex tonight. I'm really turned on.' Clear positive communication may evoke a more positive response."

Learning to initiate serves a dual positive purpose: It gets your imagination and erotic thoughts flowing, and it creates a wonderful sexual frisson between the two of you. Sex becomes a lot more interesting, fun, and meaningful when both people are stoking the initiating fires.

Now it's time to talk about the thing that every couple dreads: scheduling sex. I'm not sure why it gets such a bad rap.

CREATING YOUR SEXY SPACE: QUICK HONEY, LOCK THAT DOOR!

> **GOOD IDEA:**
> Create a time and space for sex.

There's nothing to compare when both of you are in the sex zone: Your eyes meet and, without words, you understand that getting some is inevitable. Even if the sex is up-against-the-wall fast and furious, it leaves you both with a lingering smile for days. That's how we want sex to be. It's simple, easy, and a magical experience.

Yes, of course, once in a blue moon the stars align and you both are in a great space to have sex. Most of the time, though, you have to proactively plan out how, when, and where you want to have sex.

The Dreaded Scheduling-Sex Debate

While appearing on a local TV morning show, the male host decided he needed male backup on the issue we were discussing—scheduling sex. His wingman, Rob, was a local sportscaster and known for his love of debating.

Midway through our on-air chat Rob delivered a right hook when he exclaimed, "Trina, I am scheduled up to the wazoo. I'm scheduled at work; domestic chores; and as soon as I walk through the front door with my kids. I can't fathom having to schedule one more thing, especially if that thing is sex." He made an excellent point.

And there in front of all the television viewers I let the hammer drop, "Well, Rob, from what I understand when you and your wife go up to bed, she reads her book, you watch your two late-night shows, you turn off the lights and go to sleep. You don't have any idea how to break through that monotonous habit to get a little nookie action going. Or, perhaps, you're still hoping the spontaneity gods will look sympathetically down and, poof, create hot, wild sex for you both once to twice per week. I'm sorry to tell you, it ain't gonna happen." It was like I took a pin to a balloon and he sputtered out, no answer, head hung down.

But his circumstance as well as his reaction to scheduled sex is typical. Couples already overloaded with responsibility don't want another one; they want and expect their libido to help them. However, as we've seen, it rarely does.

The "We Never Had to Schedule Sex When We Were Dating" Myth

Too many people want to believe that sex magically happened while they were dating. Did it ever occur to you sex when you were dating was the epitome of scheduling sex? Lou Paget writes in her book, *Hot*

Mammas, "Planning spontaneity is not an oxymoron.... Think about it: the majority of what we call spontaneous sex was planned, planned because at some point during these periods you knew you would be intimate because that was your intention—on the weekend, trolling a bar, your date night when single, your holiday vacation time."

As Paget points out, whether it was on weekends, vacations, during the week, you knew when you got together with your guy, you two were going to have sex. And not ironically one of the reasons sex was so great was your giddy anticipation of what was going to happen that day, or whenever you were next together.

What Does Scheduling Sex Mean for You?

There's a reason why studies have proven couples who schedule sex have better and more frequent sex. It's because it sets your brain up, builds anticipation, and is not a surprise at the end of the day. Scheduling sex means you're taking a proactive stance with your sex life instead of always being reactive. You're taking the bull by the horns (I just love the sexual innuendo that phrase implies!) and doing something about your sex.

Having sex on your terms very much needs to include scheduling sex as it requires looking at your present life situation as well as your sexual rhythm, and is especially effective when things are frantic—if you don't schedule sex during this time, it may not happen.

It goes without saying the first six or seven times you go to have your scheduled sex, it's probably not going to be a great experience for either of you—awkward, forced, and maybe with negative feelings. This is why most people give up scheduling sex before they've given it a chance.

But let's look at your sex life six months later. By creating and getting into the scheduling-sex habit, you will see how it makes a huge difference in you two staying the married-woman-sex course and keeping your precious intimacy alive.

Scheduling Date Nights, Intimacy, and Getting Lucky

Many couples feel immense pressure to perform when they start putting time aside. Especially at the start, the point of a scheduling time together isn't necessarily to have sex. It's about carving some much-needed one-on-one time with each other. Especially when you're first starting this habit, make a point to reconnect—talk about everything except your job, kids, and the daily grind. If there's an expectation hanging over your head that at the end of this date you must march into the bedroom and have sex, it might ruin your precious time together. Intimacy is your goal: if sex happens, it's a bonus. Here are some ideas:

- In-house date night. If you can't afford a babysitter, you can still have lots fun activities at your house. Strip poker isn't just for kids!
- Date-night 911. Once your kids get a bit older, have a "911" night in once per month. Take a bottle of wine and a movie into your bedroom, and shut the door. Your kids can interrupt you only with an event requiring police, paramedics, or the fire department.
- A real date night. Dinner and a movie, perhaps. Tart yourself up!
- Pick a sex day. Weekends work for many busy couples, but choose a day that works best for your schedule. Keep it the same day so you don't lose track. Make it something that both of you look forward to instead of the "weekly" duty. Lots of people love morning sex. Could there be a better way to start the day than having all of those wonderful endorphins coursing through your body?
- After a few months switch the day. Sex on Saturday mornings is a lovely, just-before-pancakes way to start your weekend. However, it can get monotonous quickly. Pick a new day and see how you can make that day work in your week.
- Get a couple calendar that's for your eyes only. Decide how often you want to plan sex (at least once every month) then take turns planning the special evening. If this seems daunting, understand that you have to plan only six nights each—per year! If you or your partner can't get the energy to plan six

nights a year, then you need to look at the other parts of your life to see why you can't make each other a priority.

- Plan a sleepover. Every couple of months, get rid of the kiddies, put on your favourite jammies, and get some finger food and a bottle of great wine. Spend the evening watching a movie, talking, taking a bath, or whatever floats your boat.

- Plan a weekend getaway. At least once a year, take two to three days away from your daily grind. It doesn't have to be exotic, but the change will have you acting like newlyweds again.

- Plan a one-week vacation at least once a year—just the two of you if it's at all financially feasible. Yes, that's seven days without the kids and everything else. If your partner truly is a priority, having some much-needed couple time once a year should not feel overwhelming.

KEY POINTS

1. Make sex about momentum, not about numbers.
2. When your mind starts to rebel, it's time to put your back into it.
3. Women are natural multi-taskers, which is fabulous in a work setting, but not so great in the bedroom. Learn to turn off your hectic day and focus on your own pleasure.
4. Commit to having sex with your partner at least once per day for seven days in a row. You'll be surprised by the results.
5. There's nothing more awkward than trying to initiate sex in a flagging, lacklustre sex life. Become an equal-opportunity initiator.
6. Spontaneous sex for busy couples is a fallacy. Consciously create a space for sex to occur.

CHAPTER 9

Making Your Married-Woman Sex Stick

"We are not interested in the possibility of defeat."

—Queen Victoria

After all of your time, effort, and hard work, it's time to play. Indulge and lavish your relationship with well-deserved love, laughter, and fun. Novelty and excitement rev up dopamine production. Therefore, the best way to keep your brain's dopamine-flooded, serotonin-starved passion alive (like at the start of your relationship) is to plan new experiences and adventures with your mate. Plus, novelty forces you to think about what you are doing, get directly involved, pay attention, take the necessary time out—instead of going on autopilot.

To keep the good times rolling, this chapter will show you how to add a little spice to your marriage. It's full of tools, ideas, and tricks to allow your imagination to run wild. Some of these ideas you'll really dig and others you won't; it's up to you to sift through and say what works and what doesn't. Feel free to dog-ear the pages and mark them up!

While reading, keep an open mind and encourage yourself to step outside your comfort zone. If it makes it easier, the two of you can divide the ideas into three categories: Absolutely; Let's See; and No Way. That way your partner will know what's cool for you.

Absolutely under no circumstance should you go through all the great ideas and do nothing about them! You've come this far, so you certainly don't want to go back to where you've been. The best news is, most of these ideas shouldn't take more than ten minutes out of your busy day.

Let's get this party started!

KEEP YOUR POSITIVE SEXUAL ATTITUDE

There is a reason the first and best "technique" to keep your sex fresh, fun, and meaningful over the long term is maintaining a positive sexual attitude. It will be the glue that will hold your sex together forevermore.

My girlfriends who enjoy sex all share this common positive sexual attitude characteristic. I've heard them say many times, "I've had a hard day/week/month and I can't wait for my man to make it up to me in bed tonight." They revel in how they will be taken care of and how nice it will be to connect with their partner. For them, the sexual experience is for their benefit, to relax and comfort them; their men are more than happy to oblige an enthusiastic sex partner.

When looking into the crystal ball at your future sex life, you need to see yourself as an eager participant. You now know what you want from your sex and have created good habits inside and outside the bedroom. Your dedication is naturally going to enhance positive thoughts toward your sex life. So begins your positive thought cycle.

The fringe benefit is that your positive sexual attitude will help maintain your self-confidence, making you sexually irresistible. You won't be able to stop the sexiness oozing out of your pores.

A Positive Sexual Attitude Does Not Mean a Perfect Relationship

Please don't believe that in order to have a positive sexual attitude you must always have smooth sailing in your relationship. Yes, obviously, it is considerably easier to connect inside the bedroom when everything in your world is running smoothly, but your marriage won't always be smooth. Likely, as soon as you hit a rough patch, your attitude toward sex will nose-dive and you'll want to shut down emotionally. If you do, and disconnect or withhold intimacy to punish, you'll undo all your hard work.

Instead, think of my sex-loving girlfriends. They also experience the normal ups and downs of relationships. Interestingly enough, they've had periods of not having sex (remember sexual rhythm?). The thing is, they understand how important sex is for their personal as well as relationship well-being. They are able to communicate with their partner about what's going on with them. No matter what, they diligently keep an intimate connection outside the bedroom so that when they are ready, it's much easier to reinitiate sex.

Your relationship will be your relationship; it will experience the same good and bad, sexual and non-sexual times. The fundamental difference will be your attitude before, during, and after each not-so-great-period in your life.

When things are rough, make sure sex and intimacy are seen as something that will help and heal you and your relationship. Keep your perspective by revisiting your goals and making sure to keep up your chosen good habits. Remind yourself that intimacy inside and outside of the bedroom is one of the few things that will keep you two connected over the long term. This will, hopefully, bring your focus back to what is going right and how you want things to be in your bedroom.

If nothing else, when you find your attitude starts going downhill, or you're having a bad day, simply fill in one of these blanks:

1. The first thing I found sexually attractive about my partner was . . .
2. One of our best sexual experiences was . . .
3. My favourite time to have sex is . . .
4. What I'd like more of in our lovemaking is . . .

A big part of this book aimed to help you turn your sexual attitude around and get rid of negative emotional baggage. Without an ongoing positive sexual attitude toward sex, your sex life will once again become fragile—and could come crashing down at any time. So please, before moving on to all the tools and techniques, have a good long think about how you will keep the positive sexual attitude alive and well in the many years to come.

LAUGH OUT LOUD IN YOUR BEDROOM

Unfortunately, sex is taken way, way, way too seriously. Serious sex completely bites the big burrito. Seriousness sucks the lifeblood out of long-term sex, and makes it boring. At this stage in the game, it's time to lighten things up. A great attitude mixed with the ability to laugh, play, and have fun will keep you enjoying sex.

When you think back to when you felt really close to your partner, it probably had everything to do with the happiness you felt. The private jokes, shared secrets, those precious times you looked into each other's eyes and laughed until it hurt. Perhaps one night you were able to sneak off, under people's noses, to have a wickedly fun quickie. Maybe it was one of those rare moments when you raced each other to the bedroom. Shared laughter and fun make it infinitely easier to stay connected.

Your Cache of Laughter Snapshots

Laughter "snapshots," or memories, remind you why you got together with your partner in the first place. Keep your eyes open for the laugh-out-loud moments. Although they can linger in our memory, these fun times are easily squashed by negative emotions. That's why it's so important to capture those wonderful moments and store them safely in your memory.

When collecting laughter snapshots, think outside the box. Look for every shared couple moment that brings a smile to your face. They could be moments with your kids or pets; when out with friends; or while vacationing. If you're keen, write down what happened in a diary; read through your memories when things aren't going as well.

Start Making Sex Adult Playtime

Reframe your thinking about sex from serious-and-sacred to adult play-time. One of my girlfriends has had a particularly bumpy life and has every right to complain and take things seriously. Yet she really (REALLY) enjoys sex. Why? She believes sex is a treat—one of the few times when she can have a good old belly laugh and play without inhibitions. In her words, "Sex is my grown-up fun time."

Keep in mind that every couple's version of fun and play is different. Early on in my career a fellow asked how he could bring fun into his relationship. Naively, I gave him a few ideas that worked for me. He phoned me a week later discouraged because his wife hated every single idea. I told him the gig was up and he would have to have a heart-to-heart to discuss what would work for them as a couple. He giddily reported back that her version of fun was a lot raunchier than he expected and was really glad he got up the nerve to have the conversation.

Since then, it has become the norm rather than the exception when couples confide being surprised (and delighted) their partner was so open to trying new and risqué things. So too with you and your partner; what you define as a fun and playful sexual experience will be different from every other couple reading this book.

The cool thing is figuring out between the two of you what's going to bring the play element into your sex. I bet both you and your part-ner are a lot more wild at heart but don't have the nerve to admit this to one another. So in no way be surprised at your willingness and enthusiasm to try new things. Plus, talking about what you want to do to each other will probably be just about as much fun as actually doing it.

Turn Feeling Foolish into Belly Laughs

Bravo to you for bringing new and exciting ideas into your bedroom. Exciting, yes, but also a bit nerve-wracking as it's never been your thing to dress up, talk dirty, or have scarves tied around your wrists. Just willing to give it a go speaks volumes to your courageousness.

And here, my friend, starts the fumbling-and-bumbling portion of your new sex life. Sometimes, when you try new playful ideas, something will go wrong. Many people hate not knowing how to execute things perfectly without looking foolish. For goodness' sake, don't get upset and stomp away. Instead, use this to lighten things up. You need to be okay with feeling silly if you're going to make your married-woman sex work. Shake it off, look each other in the eye, and laugh. Trust me, it will be part of the fun and shared smiles the next day. Isn't it great to know you have so many shared laughter snapshots to look forward to?

RANDOM ACTS OF FOREPLAY KINDNESS

Foreplay is a win-win proposition. In fact, I wish every single time the word *foreplay* was spoken a chorus of angels could be heard singing in the background. It is the holy grail of a woman's sexual desire. That's why every sex expert under the sun pleads for couples to make it happen. Simply because it is the time-tested, no-fail way to keep your sex life sensational. Foreplay revs up your sexual desire, gets your brain in gear, and fuels your mind, body, and passion. The more often you make foreplay fun, the more luscious the results of your sexual encounter.

Plan Fun
If you opted out of foreplay, pleading you were too tired and overwhelmed, toss that way of thinking. From now on, mixing it up, and bringing novelty, mystery, and fun foreplay to your sex life will be your mission. Think about how you are going to treat your partner and now he will treat you. You'll come to the sex jacked up and good to go.

The Power is in the Preparation
Don't get bent out of shape thinking you will have to spend hours

preparing "the sex scene." Foreplay really doesn't need to take a lot of effort. It's not so much what you're doing as doing something different that will change your sexual dynamic.

Don't have a clue where to start with foreplay ideas? Don't fret. There are scads of books at your local bookstore. Laura Corn's *101 Nights of Grrreat Romance* or her *101 Nights of Grrreat Sex*, have (yes, you guessed it) a combined 202 amazing ideas for hot sexy foreplay. That means if either you or your partner were to have to perform a random act of sexual kindness once a week, those two books alone would keep you in foreplay happiness for almost four years.

Getting Your Foreplay List Started

Hopefully you're a little more comfortable saying what you want sex to be. Now you need to figure out what parts of foreplay really work, are just alright, or don't do much for you. Here's a list to get you and your partner discussing and following through with what you want out of your foreplay experience.

- Kissing (remember to brush your teeth)
- Reading erotica
- Putting on sexy clothing
- Taking a nap together
- Exercising
- Spending time with yourself to relax and unwind
- Thinking about what you find sexy about your partner
- Thinking positive thoughts about your partner
- Reading a sexy novel
- Taking a shower or bath alone or together
- Stimulating yourself
- Thinking sexy thoughts
- Arousing your partner like this (insert description)
- Having a hot sexual fantasy
- Looking at your partner's naked body

Ideas to Give to Your Man

Women love romance and there's nothing wrong with that. But how you like to be romanced is unique to you. You can't expect your knight in shining armor to live up to your fairy-tale romance expectations if he doesn't know what they are. You need to tell him clearly and specifically how you would like foreplay to be. For him to get you in the mood for sex, perhaps you would like him to:

- Tell you just how sexy he thinks you are
- Talk suggestively to you
- Flirt
- Blow in your ear
- Rub his body against yours
- Tease your (insert body part)
- Put on a certain kind of clothing (describe)
- Give you a massage
- Make a special appointment on your calendar for sex
- Tell you that he desires you
- Tell you how he wants to make love to you
- Tell you what he finds sexy about you
- Take off his clothes striptease fashion
- Compliment you
- Spend close, intimate time with you
- Set a romantic scene
- Help you around the house
- Make sure you're in a relaxed mood
- Kiss you the way you like (insert description)
- Touch you the way you like (insert description)
- Wait until you are both in a good mood
- Use code words while around company because you think it's hot
- Fill your bedroom with scented candles

Great Foreplay Ideas

Here are some more really fun ideas to keep your foreplay going like the Energizer Bunny.

Tried-and-True Bath or Shower

Run a bath or shower. Lather each other up and allow your body to feel how nice his touch is.

Massage Level I

A couple can never go wrong giving each other a massage. Grab some massage oil and get to it. It doesn't matter if you're a klutz at massaging. It's all about sharing sensual touch.

Massage Level II

Once you relearn to touch and connect with your hands and bodies, take the massage up a notch. After massaging his feet, straddle his foot and give your inner labia a warm and soothing massage in the process.

Leave a Clue for Him

Leave something sexy or seductive out: a piece of underwear, a sex toy, massage oil, bubble bath to signal he's going to be getting some.

A word of caution: One woman told me she put some sexy pictures of herself in her husband's lunch. The entire morning she waited on pins and needles in giddy anticipation for his response. At two in the afternoon she called him and asked how his lunch was. He responded by saying, "It was okay. I traded my lunch with Joe." True story.

Flash Him

When he's least expecting it, flash a little skin. Maybe your entire naked body; perhaps just a small glimpse of what he can look forward to later.

Temptation Call

Don't do your routine "I just called to say I love you." Tell your partner exactly what the two of you are going to be engaged in later that day.

He Picks Your Underwear
While you're getting dressed, let him pick your underwear with the promise that later that evening he gets to take it off you.

Tell Him to Strip for You
It's not just you who needs to do a sexy striptease. Get him to shake his booty while taking off his clothes.

Slow Dance
When was the last time you put on your favourite sexy song and seductively danced together?

Change the Lighting
Candles are a no-fail way to get romantic. Take it up a notch and get a red or pink lightbulb from your local hardware store. Vamp up the sex scene by placing a scarf (careful, so it won't burn) over a lamp. It's a little cheesy, but enormously fun to pretend you're in a brothel.

Slide Around on Satin Sheets
Satin sheets add a sensual layer to the lovemaking experience. They feel great against your skin and can be a great coded signal that you want to get a little something later on.

Slowly Peel His Clothes Off
Unbutton tops slowly, stretch luxuriously while pulling a sweater over his head. Tease him, like you once did, when you undo his pants and unzip his zipper.

The number of things you can do as foreplay is limited only by your imagination (or the number of books on the bookshelf).

It's Time to Bring Your Body Into the Mix
Now that foreplay has your sexual desire piqued, it's time to get your body's sexual arousal into the program.

Let's Talk About Sex

It's time to ask yourself, what turns you on? What gets your body all juicy, wanting, and willing to have sex? The following lists are things you probably always wanted to say to your partner but never felt you could. Just talking to your partner about each and every one of these items should get your panties wet.

"Honey, When I'm Turned on I Would Like You To ..."
- Make sounds but no talking
- Talk dirty
- Say my name
- Tell me that you love me
- Sensually touch me (explain what you want)
- Pinch my nipples
- Look at me
- Touch my clitoris, inner and outer lips like this (explain)
- Play with my G-spot
- Let me play with your penis like this

"Baby, When It's Time for Sex I Would Like You To ..."
- Kiss me in these places (explain the places)
- Make sexy noises
- Be silent
- Touch me sensually in these places (explain the places)
- Stimulate my clitoris like this (make sure to show him)
- Have intercourse with me like this (describe positions)
- Make the rhythm, pressure, tempo of your thrusting like this
- Give me oral sex (let him know how you like his tongue to flick)
- Stroke me lightly on the back
- Kiss and bite me on the neck
- Show me that you are excited (explain what you mean)
- Share sex fantasies

"Sweetie, When I Want to Have More than One Orgasm . . ."
- Give me a minute then continue stimulating my clitoris
- Continue intercourse and let me ride the wave
- Stroke my G-spot with your fingers or penis
- Let me suck on your penis
- Hold me while I watch you pleasure yourself

"Honey, When the Sex Is Over Let's . . ."
- Fall asleep
- Lie in each other's arms and talk
- Kiss and caress each other
- Do it again
- Read and go to sleep
- Get up and do something else

Now that you've let him know you what you want, it's time to shake up your sex routine.

Mix and Match Your Sex Routine

Going all the way back to Chapter 1, remember that men have sex as a means to intimacy; women need intimacy as a means for sex. You need to mix up your sex routine to meet both of your needs for sex and intimacy. To do this, it's important to be aware of different love-making styles. They all have equal value, share an equal purpose, and therefore should be given equal weight.

Quickies

Remember, lovemaking doesn't always have to be a production. Quickies can satisfy the needs of the more highly sexed partner, relieve physical tension, and add more spontaneity—especially when the quickie is a stealth encounter in an unusual place like the kitchen, a walk-in closet, shower, or the backyard.

Garden Variety

This is what your usual sex looks like—fifteen to thirty minutes. You both want to experience at least a small amount of pleasure complete with orgasm, so a bit of time is required to get your juices flowing. This usually takes place in your bedroom at the beginning or end of your day. It fits in easy with your busy schedule. You can alternate two or three tried-and-true techniques with little need for negotiation. It's comfortable, cozy, and some days it's just what the doctor ordered.

Sensationally Scheduled

Leisurely sex wasn't just for the beginning of your relationship. Take a little more time—forty-five minutes to an hour. This requires some pre-thought for scene setting—such as playing music, lighting candles, dressing up, sharing a shower or bath, massage, or teasing.

Take turns setting up a special evening at least once every other month. If you take turns, it means you each plan six nights a year. And really, getting some candles from the cupboard and putting the massage oil on your nightstand isn't going tremendously out of your way to make a nice evening (see the lists of ideas from the previous sections). The delicious feelings linger long after the lovemaking has finished and allow you to happily keep up your sex momentum.

Ooh la la That Was Memorable

This kind of lovemaking is, understandably, the most difficult for the average busy couple to fit into their already overflowing schedule. Although it takes a little more time, energy, and planning, it can dramatically take you out of your comfy habits. It adds a sense of risk and playfulness to the sexual experience and can include trying new positions, sex games, sex toys, and erotica; sharing fantasies; or using various props such as food, seductive clothing, feathers, or ice—basically, all the exciting sex tips in the next section.

Even though it might not happen very often, every effort should be made to do something ooh la la at least twice a year—come on, twice a year isn't stretching things too far. It's the bond that has couples looking at each other with a secret smile for months.

THE POP-THE-HEAD-OFF FACTOR

Your new sex mantra: Monogamy isn't monotony. Just because you are with the same partner does not mean sex has to be boring. Between you and your partner, there are probably years of fun stockpiled.

Could there be anything better than going out of your way to impress and seduce your partner? How can you help him feel like he is the most special person in the world? Make a pact to pop each other's head off at least every couple of months.

People are constantly after me for the latest and greatest sex tips. So, here's my list of ways to pop the head off your partner during sex. Photocopy, dog-ear, or bookmark these next pages so you can keep coming back for more ideas.

Layering-Sex Approach

A true pop-the-head-off experience involves bringing multiple ideas into your lovemaking. It's mixing and matching a bunch of smaller sensations. For example, bringing in a sex toy is one-dimensional; bringing in a sex toy with a fantasy adds another layer. Bringing in a sex toy and sharing a fantasy while experiencing the slippery feel of satin sheets takes your encounter over the top.

There are lots of ideas here for you. The suggestions range from mild to perhaps way outside your comfort zone. Not all of these ideas will work for you. However, pop-the-head-off means pushing yourself beyond your comfort zone. Pick at least one you wouldn't normally try, do it, and then try something else.

Put a Magnet on the Fridge

A simple magnet on your fridge can be your secret signal that shows your partner how amorous you're feeling. If you place it high on the fridge, it means, "You're in luck," if it's low, it means "Don't bother asking."

Use a Naughty Getaway Weekend to Celebrate
If a sexy weekend follows a success or celebration—like you get a raise, or you've finished paying off the mortgage—you'll condition each other that good times mean equally great sex.

Become Dessert
Let him eat his favourite ice cream off your belly.

Play Doctor
Do an anatomy check on him. See how aroused you can make him and stop just before he orgasms.

Make a List of Your Favourite Sex Things
Put together a list of at least ten things you've always wanted to try. Your list could include positions, toys, lubricants, fantasy. Both of you add to the list as you discover new ideas. Taking turns, choose one of the ideas and then do it.

Dominatrix Diva
The new and improved you is ready and willing to take charge.

- Blindfold him.
- While straddling him, lift his wrists above his head.
- Tell him what you want him to do to you.

Hot and Cold
Bring hot tea and ice cubes into the bedroom. Use the ice cubes to make your mouth and tongue cold and then trace your tongue along his body. Next take a sip of hot tea and proceed to give him oral sex that he will remember for a very long time.

Sex in the Back Seat

Relive your teenage years and have sex in the back seat of your car (okay, it might be a minivan but what the heck). It will be cramped and awkward, and you'll probably laugh the entire way through.

Be His Mistress

Have an affair with your husband. Arrange to meet him at lunchtime in the bar of a hotel. If you're so inclined, buy a bottle of champagne, book a room and vamp up the fantasy.

Rent a Dirty Movie

Rent a dirty video or a pay-per-view movie with an adult theme. If you're so bold, during the movie's hot times, duplicate what the people on screen are doing while they are doing it.

Schedule Kissing Sessions

Want to get really hot and bothered? Have kissing-only sessions. It's incredibly sexy to be able to only kiss and caress each other, and get all worked up just like when you were a teenager.

Take Him on a Sex Tour

Make a point to use his body like a science experiment. Start at his head, end at his feet. Boldly find out his turn-ons and turnoffs. Then it's your turn to be the science experiment.

Restaurant Frenzy

Seek out a dimly lit restaurant with booths. While there, make sure to snuggle, play footsies, and let your hands wander. Tell your partner you're not wearing underwear and dare him to find out if you're telling the truth. Kiss passionately every time the waiter leaves your table.

Aphrodisiac Feast

Make a memorable meal of only aphrodisiacs—oysters, olives, chocolate and so much more. You can spice things up when serving by wearing only an apron and oven mitts.

Paint Each Other

Bring out your creative side. Body crayons are available at bath, novelty, or party stores. Use each other's bodies as canvases to describe what you want to have happen.

Wear Duo-balls

You insert these into your vagina to heighten stimulation. While you're out together, tell him you've got them in and you can't wait until he takes a closer look.

Put a Spin on Laundry Day

Next time you do the laundry, make a date to clean each other's clothes. You can both strip in the laundry room as you prepare the washing machine. Be sure to be on top of the washing machine once the spin cycle starts.

Take Erotic Photos

Buy a digital camera and take flattering shots of each other naked. You can always delete the evidence once you've done your photo shoot.

Keep a Photo Album

Mix photos of you and your mate on special occasions with more personal pictures. Include memories of erotic times together—a restaurant receipt, a matchbook, or a pressed flower can bring back that wonderful erotic experience.

Take Away a Sense

Turn out all the lights and pull the curtains to make the room as dark as possible. Meet each other in bed with blindfolds on. Not having a sense of sight will automatically heighten your other senses: touch, smell, hearing, and taste.

Write About Your Partner's Prowess

Write a steamy review about your partner's sexual performance. If you're good at writing, add a lot of detail like a scene from an erotic novel.

If You're Extra Confident

Use your vaginal juices as perfume. His initial attraction to you had a lot to do with your pheromones and natural scent. Doing this will make him crazy; he just won't know why.

Go Shopping for Underwear

Make a date to go shopping for sexy underwear—find out what your partner wants to see you in. When you get home, do a mini fashion show.

Dirty Dinner Party

While having a dinner party, shove him into a dark corner and completely molest him. Get him totally excited and then walk away to tend to your guests.

Have Sex with Your Clothes On

That's right, unzip his zipper, pull your panties to the side, and go crazy.

Keep Your Eyes Open During Sex

With the lights on, watch everything while having sex: Look at his face, and watch his penis move in and out.

Go Brazilian

Shave your pubic hair, leaving just a tiny "landing strip"—or go completely bare. Many women find the new sensation mind blowing.

Wake Him up Right

Surprise him one morning by giving him some great oral sex.

Give His Fingers Oral Sex

Lick and circle your tongue in and around each of his fingers. This is especially sexy if you're out for dinner and you are giving him a preview of what he can expect after supper.

Masturbate for Him

Allow him to watch you giving yourself pleasure. Let him watch you totally get into it by moaning and gyrating.

Ultimately, your sex life is your choice. Knowing you're an equal in the bedroom and actually being an equal in the bedroom are, as you've found out, two very different things. Choose fun, fresh, and meaningful sex for the rest of your life. You have nothing to lose and everything to gain.

Create a Sex Contract

To keep this wonderful sexual momentum, make sure to sit down with your partner and make a "Sex Contract." Write down the things you want to try, are willing to think about and what you expect from each other and the sexual experience. Don't know where to start? Here are some ideas you two need to discuss how you will:

- positively anticipate sexual encounters
- value emotional as much as sexual intimacy
- appreciate sex is much more than intercourse
- remember that a sexual encounter doesn't have to end in orgasm
- both enjoy affection
- both enjoy sensuality
- both enjoy playfulness
- both enjoy a sense of eroticism
- both nurture and create bridges for mutual desire
- be open minded and flexible to bring in new sexual ideas
- proactively look for ways to bring new ideas into the bedroom
- create a habit of maintaining affection and non-sexual contact

Every two or three years sit down with your partner and negotiate what you want from the sexual experience and what your new expectations are. What you want will be tied in to your present sexual rhythm, your life situation, and your changing moods.

KEY POINTS

1. The quality of your sex is directly proportional to what you focus on. Having a positive sexual attitude means always looking at your relationship for what it can be.
2. It's no secret that women need a lot more time to get into the sex groove. Make sure to have weekly random acts of foreplay kindness.
3. You need to mix it up in the bedroom so your sex never again becomes routine and stale.
4. Sex needs to be your fun time. Laugh out loud in bed and create fun ways to play.
5. Make a pact to have pop-your-partner's-head-off sex at least every couple of months.

IT'S YOUR SEX MOVE

So we've come to the end of our journey together, and now your new sex-life journey will begin. You're in the driver's seat, my friend, instead of being a passenger. I'm excited for you. Your married-woman sex is going to take you and your sex life into your twilight years. And having a lifelong love affair with your partner is about as good as it gets. Enjoy yourself and your sex!

APPENDIX 1

Is There a Best Orgasm?

For almost a hundred years, sex researchers and feminists have debated which orgasm is superior: vaginal or clitoral. Unfortunately, this debate has played with women's minds and sex lives, and left many wondering whether the orgasm they experience is the "real thing."

The ability to have a vaginal orgasm is determined by a woman's X chromosome. Approximately a third of women can consistently have a vaginal orgasm, a third sometimes have a vaginal orgasm, and a third will never experience a vaginal orgasm. In other words, the majority of woman may not consistently have vaginal orgasms, if at all.

Where it gets tricky is the "sometimes" category. Couples place a lot of pressure on the woman to have a vaginal orgasm (why too many women fake orgasm or at least the amount of positive pleasure they're experiencing during vaginal thrusting). The pressure does not allow her to be relaxed and in a good space to experience the once-in-a-while orgasm.

When I explain to men that some women will just never have a vaginal orgasm, they then ask, "Well, isn't there a finger technique or something I can do to get it to work." The answer would be no. Her inability to orgasm vaginally is, most likely, physiological and not "just in her head."

A woman's orgasm is a series of involuntary muscle contractions in the vagina, uterus, and anus that release the blood that has been stored in the erectile tissue of the genitals. Muscle contractions occur at a rate of slightly more than one per second. Generally an orgasm involves anywhere from just a few contractions to ten or fifteen of them, the intensity and duration of which varies from woman to woman.

What is the difference between a vaginal and clitoral orgasm? A vaginal orgasm is achieved via stimulation of the vaginal canal, which includes the G-spot (the female prostate), the lower interior vaginal walls, and the cervix. Vaginal orgasms are usually described as deep and relaxing, and can be followed by a profound sense of calm. Orgasm during intercourse, with fingers, with a vibrator is often less acute; however, many women prefer it for emotional reasons (e.g., it involves body-to-body contact, and holding a partner and "giving" oneself to him at the same time). Masters and Johnson reported that during a vaginal orgasm the internal organs are pushed downward, contracting the upper half of the vagina.

The clitoral orgasm, the most common, is achieved by direct stimulation of the clitoris by sex toys, the partner's fingers or tongue, or masturbation. Clitoral orgasms are more intense because stimulation is localized and purposely guided. They are typically described as "higher" and "intense," and can be accompanied by a sense of overstimulation. Masters and Johnson reported stronger contraction spasms and higher rates of heartbeat during clitoral orgasm, especially during masturbation, and many women confirmed that they had their best orgasms when alone. The research showed that regardless of what kind of orgasm a woman experiences, she will have the same sexual bodily response.

THE CLITORIS AND VAGINA

The Clitoris

The clitoris, the female sex organ, is roughly comparable to the penis as it is made up of the same type of tissue, and is lined with the same sensitive nerve endings. Unlike the penis, however, the clitoris serves no other function than to provide sexual pleasure and can be difficult to see without the aid of a mirror. It may be so concealed that it can be seen only when the labia majora (outer lips of the vagina) are separated (see diagram on page 207).

Located above the vaginal and urethral openings, the clitoris is structurally connected to the labia minora (inner lips of the vagina). The visible glans (rounded head) of the clitoris is only the outward and visible manifestation of the erectile tissue's extensive structure, which pads the pubic bone.

For many women, the most important site of sexual sensitivity is the clitoral area. Sex therapist Helen Singer Kaplan found two-thirds of her research group preferred and responded more readily to clitoral than vaginal stimulation. This is because the density of nerve endings in the clitoris is far greater than the vagina. In fact, the entire surrounding area, including above, to the sides, and below is generally highly sensitive to sexual stimulation.

The Vagina

The vagina begins at the opening and extends about 3 to 5 inches inside, ending at the cervix, or neck of the uterus. It consists of three layers of tissue. The first surface layer, the mucosa, can be touched, and consists of mucous membranes similar to the lining of the mouth. Unlike the smooth surface of the mouth lining, the mucosa contains folds and wrinkles. The second layer of tissue is muscle concentrated mostly around the outer third of the vagina. The third, innermost layer consists of fibrous tissue that connects to other anatomical structures.

In the sexually unstimulated state, the vagina is shaped like a flattened tube, the sides of which are collapsed on each other. It is not a continually open space, or "hole" as people often think: rather it is a "potential" space. Due to its muscular tissue, the vagina can expand and contract, like a balloon, allowing a baby to pass through during childbirth, or adjust to fit snugly around a tampon, finger, or any-size penis.

The outer one-third of the vagina near the opening (see diagram on page 209) contains nearly 90 per cent of the vaginal nerve endings and therefore is much more sensitive to touch than the inner two-thirds of the vagina.

During sexual excitement, droplets of fluid appear along the vaginal walls and eventually cover the sides of the vagina completely. The vaginal tissue does not contain any secretory glands itself; however, it is loaded with blood vessels, which when engorged with blood as a result of sexual arousal, press against the tissue, forcing natural tissue fluids through the walls of the vagina.

Vaginal lubrication typically decreases as women age, but this is a natural physical change that does not normally mean there is any physical or psychological problem. After menopause, the body produces less estrogen, which causes the vaginal walls to thin significantly. The vagina also tends to become slightly shorter and narrower, and it takes longer to produce even a reduced amount of lubrication. The vagina also loses its ability to expand as easily during sexual excitement.

An orgasm is preceded by moistening of the vaginal wall and an enlargement of the clitoris due to increased blood flow trapped in the clitoris's spongy tissue. As a woman comes closer to orgasm, the clitoris moves under the clitoral hood, and the labia minora become a darker pink. As orgasm becomes imminent, the vagina decreases in size by about 30 per cent and the walls become congested with blood. Involuntary actions occur, including vocalizations and muscular spasms in other areas of the body. A woman experiences full orgasm when her uterus, vagina, and pelvic muscles undergo a series of rhythmic contractions.

When the orgasm is finished, the clitoris re-emerges from under the clitoral hood, returning to its original size in less than ten minutes, and the woman feels a general sense of euphoria.

SIGMUND FREUD'S VIEW
ON THE FEMALE ORGASM

Arguably, no one has had more impact on the female orgasm than Sigmund Freud. In 1905, Freud theorized that the clitoral orgasm was an adolescent phenomenon, and upon reaching puberty a woman's "proper" response changed from clitoral to vaginal orgasms. Clitoral stimulation was immature and masculine in nature; therefore, women needed to abandon clitoral pleasures and affect a transfer, achieving orgasm vaginally. Freud believed that once a woman finally submitted to the sexual act, the excitement she once felt in her clitoris would be transferred to her vagina.

Although Freud did not provide evidence supporting this basic assumption, the consequences of the theory were greatly elaborated thereafter. It is interesting to note that Freud's followers adhered to his theories more rigidly than did Freud himself. Some scholars believe that when he came up with this theory, he was trying to provide a explanation of why some women have different types of orgasms. Nevertheless, his theory that the clitoris was an infantile source of pleasure would establish the controversy to this day.

ALFRED KINSEY'S RESEARCH
ON THE FEMALE ORGASM

In 1953, Alfred Kinsey's *Sexual Behavior in the Human Female* further contributed to the clitoral versus vaginal orgasm debate. When Kinsey brought female sexuality out of the closet, a great deal of open discussion centred around the female orgasm. In effect, before Kinsey many women felt under intense pressure to have a vaginal orgasm.

Kinsey's findings disproved Freud's belief that the majority of women were "frigid" because they weren't able to have an orgasm. In fact, nine out of the ten women contributing their sexual histories to Kinsey's study reported having an orgasm by the age of thirty-five.

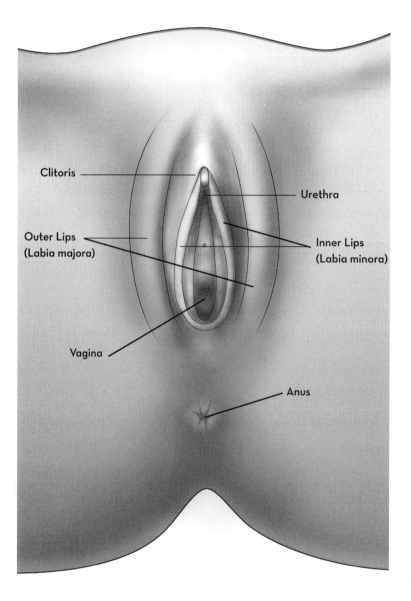

Masturbation proved to be the surest route to orgasm, with 95 per cent surveyed achieving success. Among the married women surveyed, the major difference between those who responded with orgasm always or almost always, as opposed to those who rarely or never achieved orgasm, was their premarital sexual experience. Among women who had had orgasms before marriage, 45 per cent experienced orgasm in all or almost all of their sexual encounters during their first year of marriage.

Kinsey concluded that the problem was not the inability of women to achieve orgasm. The problem was that the majority of women failed to achieve orgasm during intercourse. Therefore, the most probable cause of female frigidity in marriage is the repression of sexual responsiveness, and especially the repression of masturbation, in girls and young women before marriage.

WILLIAM MASTERS AND VIRGINIA JOHNSON'S RESEARCH ON THE FEMALE ORGASM

Other significant contributors to the study of women's sexuality were William Masters and Virginia Johnson, who published their pivotal research in *Human Sexual Response* in 1966. They set out to determine the physiological stages leading up to and following orgasm. They found that vaginal and clitoral orgasms follow the same stages of physical response.

As part of the research, the team filmed women's vaginal reactions during their sexual-response cycle using a transparent plastic "penis" camera. From this, Masters and Johnson developed the notion of four phases of sexual response, and then proceeded to treat them as independently measurable entities. Masters and Johnson described the anatomical changes in the clitoris and surrounding tissues during sexual excitement and orgasm. They found clitoral erection present in 50 per cent of women.

Masters and Johnson compared in detail orgasms following clitoral stimulation with orgasms following vaginal stimulation in the absence

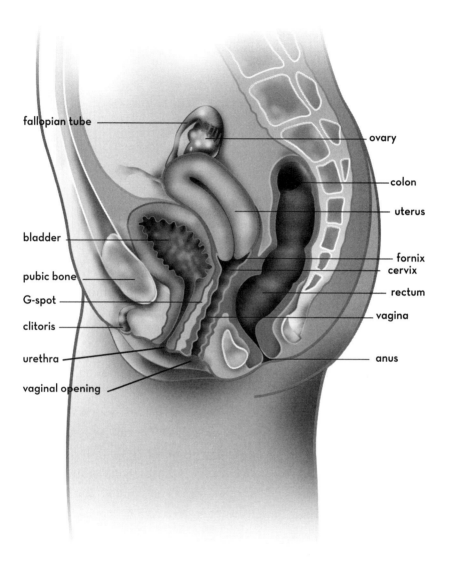

fallopian tube

ovary

colon

uterus

bladder

fornix
cervix

pubic bone

rectum

G-spot

vagina

clitoris

urethra

anus

vaginal opening

of a partner. When studied objectively in this manner, supposed clitoral and vaginal orgasms proved to be physiologically indistinguishable. Feminists adopted the researchers' standpoint on clitoral orgasm; indeed, some believed the vaginal orgasm was a patriarchal mirage created for men's convenience. The clitoral-only orgasm school of thought became an article of faith in some feminist circles.

CONCLUSION

Is there a best kind of orgasm? No.

Physiologically, an orgasm is an orgasm regardless of the stimulation: masturbation, intercourse, oral, or otherwise. The subjective experience may differ, but the physiological cycle a woman goes through as she builds sexual tension, reaches orgasm, and returns to the initial resting place is the same for all women.

Although all orgasms are equal, women do report different sensations according to whether they are being penetrated or masturbated. Some women do have orgasms that they describe as "vaginal" from penetrative intercourse, which are distinct from those achieved through clitoral stimulation. It can be argued the new focus on the clitoris has eluded the contribution to sexual pleasure and orgasm of the sensitive erectile tissues of the rest of the vulva.

The good news is that, after all of this debate, women can claim several different kinds of climax. Some women are able to orgasm through pressure on the G-spot or pressure on the cervix by fingers or penis. Many women report that some form of vaginal stimulation is essential to experience a complete orgasm, in addition to or in lieu of clitoral stimulation. Recent anatomical research has pointed toward a connection between intra-vaginal tissues and nerve endings on the one hand, and the clitoris on the other. The most important thing is, all orgasms are terrific. It does not matter how a woman climaxes, so long as she enjoys herself in the process.

APPENDIX 2

Female Sexual-Response Cycle

The female sexual-response cycle comprises four phases: excitement, plateau, orgasm, and resolution. There is no distinct beginning or end to each phase; each is part of a continuous process of sexual response.

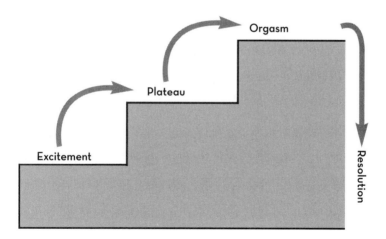

PHASE 1: EXCITEMENT

General characteristics of the excitement phase, which can last from a few minutes to several hours, include the following:

- Muscle tension increases.
- Heart rate quickens and breathing is accelerated.
- Skin may become flushed (blotches of redness appear on the chest and back).
- Nipples become hardened or erect.
- Blood flow to the genitals increases, resulting in swelling of the clitoris and labia minora (inner lips).
- Vaginal lubrication begins.
- The breasts become fuller and the vaginal walls begin to swell.

PHASE 2: PLATEAU

General characteristics of the plateau phase, which extends to the brink of orgasm, include the following:

- The changes begun in phase 1 are intensified.
- The vagina continues to swell from increased blood flow, and the vaginal walls turn dark purple.
- The clitoris becomes highly sensitive (may even be painful to touch) and retracts under the clitoral hood to avoid direct stimulation.
- Breathing, heart rate, and blood pressure continue to increase.
- Muscle spasms may begin in the feet, face, and hands.
- Muscle tension increases.

PHASE 3: ORGASM

Orgasm is the climax of the sexual-response cycle. It is the shortest of the phases and generally lasts only a few seconds. Its general characteristics include the following:

- Involuntary muscle contractions begin.
- Blood pressure, heart rate, and breathing are at their highest rates, with a rapid intake of oxygen.
- Muscles in the feet spasm.
- There is a sudden, forceful release of sexual tension.
- The muscles of the vagina contract. The uterus also undergoes rhythmic contractions.
- A rash or "sex flush" may appear over the entire body.

PHASE 4: RESOLUTION

During this phase, the body slowly returns to its normal level of functioning, and swelled and erect body parts return to their previous size and colour. This phase is marked by a general sense of well-being, enhanced intimacy, euphoria, and, often, fatigue. Some women are capable of a rapid return to the orgasm phase with further sexual stimulation and may experience multiple orgasms.

RESOURCES

BOOKS

Relationships

Corn, Laura. *101 Nights of Grrreat Romance: Secret Sealed Seductions for Fun-Loving Couples*. Los Angeles: Park Avenue Publishers, 2005.

Corn, Laura. *101 Nights of Grrreat Sex: Secret Sealed Seductions for Fun-Loving Couples*. Los Angeles: Park Avenue Publishers, 2005.

Corn, Laura. *The Great American Sex Diet: Where the Only Thing You Nibble on ... Is Your Partner*. New York: HarperCollins Publishers Inc., 2001.

Gottman, John, and Nan Silver. *The Seven Principles for Making Marriage Work*. New York: Three Rivers Press, 2004.

Hooper, Anne. *Kama Sutra for 21st Century Lovers*. New York: DK Publishing Inc., 2007.

Keesling, Barbara. *All Night Long: How to Make Love to a Man Over 50*. New York: HarperCollins Publishers, 2000.

Love, Patricia and Jo Robinson. *Hot Monogamy*. New York, Dutton, 1997.

McCarthy, Barry and Emily. *Rekindling Desire: A Step-by-Step Program to Help Low-Sex and No-Sex Marriages*. New York: Brunner-Routledge, 2003.

Perel, Esther. *Mating in Captivity: Reconciling the Erotic and the Domestic*. New York: HarperCollins Publishers, 2006.

Schnarch, David. *Passionate Marriage: Keeping Love and Intimacy Alive in Committed Relationships*. New York: W.W. Norton and Company, 1997.

Wachtel, Ellen. *We Love Each Other But...: Simple Secrets to Strengthen Your Relationship and Make Love Last*. New York: St. Martin's Griffin, 1999.

Weiner Davis, Michele. *The Sex-Starved Marriage: Boosting Your Marriage Libido—A Couple's Guide*. New York: Simon & Schuster Paperbacks, 2004.

Sex and Motherhood

Paget, Lou. *Hot Mammas: The Ultimate Guide to Staying Sexy Throughout Your Pregnancy and Months Beyond*. Mississauga, ON: Doubleday Canada, 2006.

Raskin, Valerie. *Great Sex for Moms: Ten Steps to Nurturing Passion While Raising Kids*. New York: Fireside, 2002.

Seamans, Anne, and Cathy Winks. *The Mother's Guide to Sex*. Makawao, Maui: Inner Ocean Publication, Inc., 2004.

Women's Sexuality

Brizendine, Louann. *The Female Brain*. New York: Morgan Road Books, 2006.

Davidson, Joy. *Fearless Sex: A Babe's Guide to Overcoming Your Romantic Obsessions and Getting the Sex Life You Deserve*. Gloucester, MA: Fair Winds Press, 2004.

Foley, Sallie, Sally A. Kope, and Dennis P. Sugrue. *Sex Matters for Women: A Complete Guide to Taking Care of Your Sexual Self*. New York: The Guildford Press, 2002.

Hall, Kathryn. *Reclaiming Your Sexual Self*. Hoboken, NJ: John Wiley & Sons. 2004.

Quilliam, Susan. *The Woman's Complete Illustrated Guide to Sex*. Gloucester, MA: Fair Winds Press, 2003.

Women's Orgasm

Barbach, Lonnie. *For Yourself: The Fulfillment of Female Sexuality*. New York: Signet, 2000.

Cattrall, Kim, and Mark Levinson. *Satisfaction: The Art of the Female Orgasm*. New York: Warner Books, 2003.

Dodson, Betty. *Sex for One: The Joy of Selfloving*. New York: Three Rivers Press, 1996.

Winks, Cathy. *The Good Vibrations Guide: The G-Spot*. San Francisco: Down There Press, 1998.

Perimenopause and Menopause

Prior, Jerilynn. *Estrogen's Storm Season: stories of perimenopause*. Vancouver: Centre for Menstrual Cycle and Ovulation Research (CEMCOR), 2005.

Sheehy, Gail. *Sex and the Seasoned Woman: Pursuing the Passionate Life*. New York: Random House, 2006.

Wiley, T.S. with Julie Tanguchi and Bent Formby. *Sex, Lies and Menopause: The Shocking Truth About Hormone Replacement Therapy.* New York: William Morrow, 2003.

Male Sexuality
Zilbergeld, Bernie. *The New Male Sexuality: The Truth about Men, Sex and Pleasure.* New York: Bantam Books, 1999.

WEBSITES

Finding a Therapist
American Psychological Association (APA)
750 First Street N.E.
Washington, D.C. 20002-4242
Telephone: (800) 374-2721/(202) 336-5500
Referral Information: (800) 964-2000
www.apa.org
APA's website links to provincial and state websites that refer to local psychological associations.

American Association for Marriage and Family Therapy (AAMFT)
112 South Alfred Street
Alexandria, WA 22314-3061
Telephone: (703) 838-9808
Fax: (703) 838-9805
www.aamft.org
AAMFT does not offer referrals via its website but it does have a locator.

American Association of Sex Educators, Counselors and Therapists (AASECT)
P.O. Box 1960
Ashland, VA 23005-1960
Telephone: (804) 752-0026

Fax: (804) 752-0056
www.aasect.org

Sexual Information
American Association of Sex Educators, Counselors and Therapists
(AASECT)
P.O. Box 1960
Ashland, VA 23005-1960
Telephone: (804) 752-0026
Fax: (804) 752-0056
www.aasect.org

The Kinsey Institute for Research in Sex, Gender and Reproduction
313 Morrison Hall
Indiana University
Bloomington, IN 47405
Telephone: (812) 855-7686
www.kinseyinstitute.org

The New View Campaign
163 Third Avenue, Suite 183
New York, NY 10003
Telephone: (212) 533-2774
Fax: (212) 254-5922
www.fsd-alert.org

Sexuality Information and Education Council of Canada (SIECCAN)
850 Coxwell Avenue
Toronto, Ontario
M4C 5R1
Telephone: (416) 466-5304
Fax: (416) 778-0785
www.sieccan.org

Sexuality Information and Education Council of the United States
(sieccus)
90 John Street, Suite 704
New York, NY 10038
Telephone: (212) 819-9770
Fax: (212) 819-9776
www.siecus.org

Society for Sexuality
www.sexuality.org

Personality Test
www.kolbe.com

Menopause

Centre for Menstrual Cycle and Ovulation Research (cemcor)
The Gordon and Leslie Diamond Health Care Centre
Room 4111, 4th Floor
2775 Laurel Street,
Vancouver, BC
v5z 1m9
Telephone: (604) 875-5927
Fax: (604) 875-5915
www.cemcor.ubc.ca

American Menopause Foundation
350 Fifth Avenue, Suite 2822
New York, NY 10118
Telephone: (212) 714-2398
www.americanmenopause.org

North American Menopause Society
P.O. Box 94527
Cleveland, OH 44101

Telephone: (440) 442-7550
Fax: (440) 442-2660
www.menopause.org

EROTICA AND SEX TOYS

Listed are well-run websites that do not give pornographic spam.

A Little More Interesting
Calgary, AB
www.alittlemoreinteresting.com

Come As You Are
Toronto, ON
www.comeasyouare.com

Eve's Garden
New York, NY
www.evesgarden.com

Forever Pleasure
Edmonton, AB
www.foreverpleasure.com

Good Vibrations
San Francisco, CA
www.goodvibes.com

Toys in Babeland
New York, LA, and Seattle
www.babeland.com

ACKNOWLEDGEMENTS

It's so cliché to compare writing a book to having baby. But as I pushed out this book then pushed out my son a few weeks later, I have seen first-hand that it's true. It does take a village to create a great book.

Here's my book's village.

Thank you to my agent Robert Mackwood for sticking by me and giving great guidance.

Thank you to my team of editors: Carol Harrison at Key Porter Books, who held my hand and took a very insecure me through the publishing process; Jill Lambert; Dani LeClaire; and Karen Rolfe, who gave fabulous feedback.

Thank you to my parents Lynn Loree, Sandy Read, and Walter Read; as well to Keith Hannah, Lorna McLaren, Jolie Engelbrecht, Jennifer and Patrick Knox, Monty Loree, Brian Parker, and Susan Naylen-Sorrell, who all listened to my incessant whinging through the writing and editing processes, and gave me loads of encouragement.

The biggest thanks to my husband Dennis for his never-ending and unshakable support.

INDEX